Artificial Intelligence Proves Catholicism is True

Artificial Intelligence Proves Catholicism is True

David L. Gray

Saint Dominic's Media
Warren, Ohio

Artificial Intelligence Proves Catholicism is True

Published by Saint Dominic's Media, Inc., Warren, Ohio. The Mission of Saint Dominic's Media is to acquire, develop, produce, market, and distribute works of non-fiction and fiction that reflect the Dominican spirit of a life devoted to liturgical prayer, study of sacred truth, and zeal for the salvation of souls, for an audience that is seeking a richer, deeper spiritual life while living in the world. We seek to do all things Deum verum, for the truth of God. www.saintdominicsmedia.com

Printed in the United States of America

26 27 28 29 30 31 32   10 9 8 7 6 5 4 3 2 1

BISAC Categories:
REL067030 (Catholic)
REL067080 (Apologetics)
PHI022000 (Philosophy / Religious)

ISBN-13: 979-8-9857040-6-8 (Paperback)

Contents

Introduction

I posed fifteen questions, plus one follow-up, to Claude (Opus 4.7), Anthropic's large language model. The account was new; Claude had no prior context about my identity or beliefs. The goal was simple: if a reasoning system were asked unbiased questions about the existence of a necessary being and the rational structure of communication from such a being, where would the chain of reasoning lead?

The chapters that follow record those exchanges verbatim, with the exception of the insertion of *METHODOLOGY* following the original question. The methodology of the question intends to inform the reader of the purpose of the question in the sequence. Also note that any of the responses that are in bold and any punctuation errors were also generated by Claude. Excluding the format and methodology, all of my questions and Claude Opus 4.7 answers are verbatim to the original chat history and can be made available upon request.

Question 1: Is it logically possible for a non-contingent being to exist?

Question:

Is it logically possible for a non-contingent being to exist?

METHODOLOGY, Foundation. This question establishes the logical possibility of the entire inquiry. Before asking what a non-contingent being is like, we must establish that such a being is not self-contradictory. The argument proceeds by reductio: if everything were contingent, the chain of dependence would have no terminus, which is incoherent. This question opens the only door through which the rest of the chain can pass. If 'no' is rational here, the inquiry ends. It frames everything downstream.

Claude Opus 4.7

This is a classic question in modal metaphysics and philosophy of religion. Let's work through it carefully.

Definitions first

A **contingent being** is one that *could have failed to exist*; its existence depends on something outside itself. You, this conversation, the Earth: all contingent.

A **non-contingent being** (often called a **necessary being**) is one that *could not have failed to exist*; its non-existence is impossible. It exists in every possible world, or equivalently, there is no possible world in which it is absent.

Is it logically possible?

The short answer is: there is no obvious logical contradiction in the concept, but whether it is genuinely possible is deeply contested. Here's why:

The case that it IS logically possible

1. **No formal contradiction.** The definition, "a being whose non-existence is impossible," does not produce a syntactic contradiction the way "a married bachelor" does. The concept is at least coherent on its face.
2. **Mathematical analogy.** Many philosophers argue that abstract objects like numbers or logical truths are non-contingent: the number 2 doesn't happen to exist, it couldn't not exist. If you accept this, non-contingent existence is already instantiated.
3. **Conceivability argument.** We can clearly *conceive* of such a being without running into immediate contradiction, which is at least weak evidence of possibility.
4. **Modal ontological arguments** (Plantinga, etc.) leverage S5 modal logic to argue: *if* a necessary being is possible (i.e., exists in some possible world), then by the logic of necessity, it exists in *all* possible worlds, including the actual one. So possibility collapses into actuality for necessary beings.

The case that it is NOT logically possible (or that the concept is problematic)

1. **The "Kant objection":** Existence is not a predicate. You cannot define something into existence. Saying

a being "necessarily exists" may be a grammatical sentence that fails to pick out a coherent metaphysical property.

2. **Hume's challenge:** Whatever can be conceived to exist can be conceived not to exist. On this view, necessity is a feature of propositions and logical relations, not of independently existing beings. A "necessary being" would be a category error.
3. **The conceivability-possibility gap:** Just because we can conceive of a necessary being without obvious contradiction doesn't mean one is genuinely metaphysically possible. Our conceivability is an imperfect guide.
4. **Parody arguments (inspired by Gaunilo):** If the logic works for a maximally great being, couldn't it work for a "necessarily existing pizza"? The challenge is showing why some entities can be necessary and others can't, without begging the question.
5. **The question of self-explanation**: A necessary being is often said to be *self-explanatory* or to exist *a se* (from itself). Critics argue this is incoherent; nothing explains its own existence in the way required.

The deeper issue: two senses of "necessity."

Much hinges on whether **necessity** is:

- **Logical/analytic necessity, true by definition alone (like "all bachelors are unmarried").** A necessary being in this sense would be one whose existence follows from its essence by pure logic, which many find incoherent for a concrete entity.
- **Metaphysical necessity**, true in all possible worlds, even if not analytically provable. This is weaker and more permissive. Most contemporary defenders of necessary beings (Plantinga, Swinburne) mean this.

On the metaphysical reading, the concept is at least *coherent enough* to be a serious philosophical position. On the strict logical reading, the concept faces severe skeptical pressure.

Summary

Position	**View**
Thomists / Classical Theists	Yes, God exists necessarily; the concept is not only possible but actual
Plantinga-style modal theists	Yes, possibly possible, and if so, actual (via S5)
Humeans / empiricists	No, necessity applies only to propositions, not beings
Kantians	Problematic, existence isn't a predicate; the concept misfires
Platonists	Yes, but only for abstract objects, not concrete beings

The majority view in contemporary analytic philosophy of religion is that the concept of a necessary being is **logically coherent** (i.e., not formally contradictory), even among many atheist philosophers who simply deny that any such being *actually* exists. The real battle is not logical possibility but **whether possibility entails actuality** for such a being, and **whether the concept is genuinely meaningful**, which remain live and unresolved debates.

Question 2: If a non-contingent being exists, what properties would it logically have?

Question:

If a non-contingent being exists, what properties would it logically have?

METHODOLOGY, Deductive unpacking. Having established the possibility (Q. 1), we now derive properties strictly from the concept of non-contingency itself, not from revelation, scripture, or tradition. Each property (eternity, immutability, simplicity, unity) is shown to follow because its negation would reintroduce contingency. This is pure metaphysical analysis. This sets up Q. 3 by making the question of intellect/will the next logical attribute to test.

Claude Opus 4.7

This is where the metaphysics gets really rich. If we grant that a non-contingent (necessary) being exists, we can try to derive its properties through pure reasoning, asking what *must* be true of something whose non-existence is impossible. Many of these properties follow from each other in a chain of logical entailments.

The Core Derivations

1. Necessary Existence (by definition)

This is the starting point. The being exists in every possible world. Its existence has no external cause or condition; it simply *cannot* fail to be. Everything else follows from unpacking what this means.

---

2. Aseity (Self-Subsistence)

A necessary being cannot depend on anything external for its existence, because if it did, its existence would be *contingent* on that thing. Therefore, it must exist *a se*, from itself, through itself, as its own sufficient reason. It is ontologically self-sufficient in an absolute sense.

---

3. Uncaused

If it were caused by something else, its existence would depend on that cause, making it contingent. So it must be uncaused, the terminus of any causal chain, not a link within one. This is why classical traditions call it the *First Cause* or *Unmoved Mover*.

---

4. Eternal / Atemporal (or Omnitemporal)

Time is the measure of change and contingent process. If the necessary being were *in* time in the ordinary sense, it would be subject to temporal conditions; it would exist *at* moments rather than simply and absolutely. Two possibilities follow:

- **Atemporal**: it exists entirely outside time (the classical view, Boethius, Aquinas)
- **Omnitemporal**: it exists at *all* times necessarily, without beginning or end

Either way, it cannot have begun or cease to exist, since that would imply contingency.

---

5. Immutable (Unchanging)

Change involves moving from one state to another, gaining or losing properties. But any such change would imply:

- the being *lacked* something before the change (imperfection/dependence), or
- the being *could* be other than it is (contingency of its properties)

A necessary being's properties must themselves be necessary. It cannot be otherwise than it is. This leads to the classical doctrine of divine immutability.

---

6. Simple (Non-Composite)

This is one of the most striking derivations. If the being were composed of parts, whether physical, metaphysical, or even the distinction between *essence* and *existence*, then:

- those parts would be prior to the whole
- the whole would depend on the parts for its existence
- the being's existence would be contingent on the parts combining

Therefore, a necessary being must be **absolutely simple**, not assembled from anything. Its essence just *is* its existence. There is no gap between what it is and that it is. (This is the doctrine of **Divine Simplicity** in classical theology.)

---

7. Infinite / Unlimited

Any limitation on a being implies a boundary, something it is *not*, some property it *lacks*. But a lack implies dependence on external factors that determine what falls inside or outside its nature. A necessary being cannot be limited by anything external to itself. Therefore, it is in some sense **infinite**, not bounded by anything outside it.

---

8. Uniqueness (There Can Only Be One)
Suppose there were two necessary beings, A and B. What would distinguish them? Any distinguishing property would have to be something one has, and the other lacks, but a lack implies limitation, and limitation implies contingency (see above). More formally: if both are truly necessary and unlimited, there is no metaphysical "room" for differentiation. The necessary being must be one, a conclusion reached by Aquinas, Spinoza, and others through very different routes.

---

9. The Ground of Contingent Existence
If contingent things exist, they require an explanation for their existence. The necessary being, as the only self-explanatory entity, must ultimately be the ground or source of whatever contingent things exist. It functions as the ontological foundation of the contingent order. This doesn't automatically mean it created contingent beings (that requires further argument), but it must, in some sense, sustain or account for them.

---

10. Power (Omnipotence, with qualifications)
As the uncaused ground of all contingent existence, the necessary being must have the capacity to bring about or sustain whatever contingently exists. This implies vast, perhaps unlimited, causal power. However, strict omnipotence (can do *absolutely anything*) is more contested:

can it make a necessary truth false? Can it make itself not exist? These push into paradox. A cleaner formulation: it has **maximal power** consistent with its own necessary nature.

---

11. Does it have Mind or Will? (The Contested Step)

The properties above follow fairly tightly from necessity alone. But classical theology goes further and attributes **intellect** and **will** to the necessary being. The arguments here are less decisive:

- **From simplicity**: if the being is simple and its essence = existence = goodness, and if understanding is a perfection, it must possess understanding eminently
- **From agency**: if it is the source of a contingent, structured world, some kind of intentional ordering seems required, brute causation alone seems insufficient to explain *why this* world rather than another
- **From the nature of infinity**: a being unlimited in actuality would seem to include cognitive and volitional perfections

But critics (like Spinoza) argue the necessary being need not be *personal* at all; it may be more like a necessary *ground of being* than a mind. This is where **theism** and **pantheism/monism** diverge.

The Property Map

NECESSARY EXISTENCE

```
│
├──► Aseity (self-subsistent)
│     │
│     └──► Uncaused
│
├──► Eternal / Atemporal
│
├──► Immutable
│
├──► Simple (non-composite)     ──► Unique
(only one)
│     │
│     └──► Infinite / Unlimited
│
└──► Ground of contingent beings   ──►
Maximal Power
              │
   (contested) └──► Intellect &
Will
```

Important Caveats

Several things do **not** straightforwardly follow, and are subject to serious dispute:

Property	**Status**
Moral goodness / omnibenevolence	Requires further argument (from perfection or from the nature of being)
Personhood	Highly contested, depends on what "person" means
Creator (ex nihilo)	A metaphysical option, not a logical necessity
Providence / involvement in history	Far beyond what logic alone delivers
Responsiveness to prayer	Requires contingent will, which conflicts with strict immutability

---

The Fundamental Tension

Many of these properties sit in **internal tension** with each other:

- **Simplicity** + **Power**: How can a simple, undifferentiated being *do* different things?
- **Immutability** + **Will**: Genuine willing seems to involve before/after states, change
- **Aseity** + **Creation**: If the being is fully self-sufficient, why or how does it produce anything contingent?
- **Uniqueness** + **Relation**: Can a strictly simple, unique being stand in *real relations* to contingent things?

These tensions are not necessarily fatal, classical theologians spent centuries developing sophisticated responses. But they reveal that the concept of a necessary being, while perhaps logically coherent, generates formidable internal pressure the moment we try to elaborate its properties in full detail.

The remarkable thing is how much follows from *necessity alone*, long before we introduce revelation, religious experience, or tradition. The logic of non-contingency is surprisingly productive and surprisingly demanding.

Follow-up Question

You did not offer a conclusion to the question.

Claude Opus 4.7

You're right, and I should have.

Conclusion

If a non-contingent being exists, it would logically possess the following core properties, each entailed by the previous:

It would be **self-subsistent, uncaused, eternal, immutable, simple, infinite, and unique.** These properties form a tight logical chain: necessity rules out dependence, dependence rules out causation, causation rules out temporal origin, and so on through to uniqueness. You cannot consistently affirm necessary existence and deny these properties without contradiction.

This derived profile is strikingly close to what classical theology calls **God**, specifically the God of Aquinas, Maimonides, and Avicenna, rather than the more personal, relational God of popular religion. That convergence is philosophically significant: it suggests that *if* the ontological or cosmological arguments succeed in establishing a necessary being at all, they deliver something with genuine metaphysical weight, not a thin or trivial conclusion.

However, the honest conclusion must include two limits:

1. **First**, the properties that matter most to religious believers, goodness, personhood, love, and creative intent, do *not* follow with the same logical tightness. They require additional premises that are contested.
2. **Second, the internal tensions among the derived properties (immutability vs. will, simplicity vs. power, aseity vs. creation) are real and unresolved. They don't prove the concept is incoherent, but they do mean the necessary being, fully described, strains the limits of what our concepts can coherently handle.**

So the conclusion is this: **the existence of a non-contingent being would be logically explosive**, a single necessary being would, by pure entailment, have to be the eternal, simple, infinite, unique ground of all contingent reality. But whether that being is also *good, personal,* or *caring* remains a further question that logic alone cannot settle.

Question 3: Would such a being be capable of intelligence or will?

Question:

Would such a being be capable of intelligence or will?

METHODOLOGY, Bridge from impersonal to personal. Questions 1–2 leave open whether the non-contingent being is a mere principle (like a brute necessity) or a personal reality. This question forces the issue by asking whether intellect and will are compatible with or required by the properties already derived. If the being is the ground of all actuality, it cannot lack the actualities found in its effects (the principle of proportionate causality). This is the inflection point that makes communication (Q. 5+) coherent.

Claude Opus 4.7

This is precisely where the logical chain becomes most strained, and most interesting. The question cuts to the heart of whether the necessary being of metaphysics is the same as the God of religion.

The Case FOR Intelligence and Will

1. The Argument from Perfection

If the necessary being is truly infinite and unlimited, then any genuine perfection must belong to it, because a lack of any perfection would imply a limitation, and limitation implies contingency. Intelligence and will are unambiguously perfections, they represent a *higher* mode of being than their absence. A stone is less than an animal; an animal is less than a mind. Therefore an unlimited being must possess these perfections, at minimum *eminently*, meaning it contains whatever is real and positive in them, even if in a mode we cannot fully conceive.

2. The Argument from Ordered Contingency

The contingent world is not a formless blob, it is structured, lawful, and intelligible. If the necessary being is the ground of contingent existence, it must in some sense account for *why this particular order* rather than chaos or nothing. Brute, mindless causation seems insufficient to explain specific, fine-grained structure. Some form of intentional ordering, which implies intelligence, seems required. This is essentially the **teleological pressure** within cosmological reasoning.

3. The Argument from Self-Knowledge

A being that is purely actual, infinite, and simple would, by the classical doctrine, *be* its own intelligible content. There is nothing hidden from it, no opacity in its nature. Aquinas argues that intellect just *is* the capacity of a being to be other things intentionally, without becoming them materially. A being that *is* pure actuality and simplicity would know itself perfectly and thereby, as ground of all being, know everything that flows from it. Intelligence here is not an added faculty but a consequence of what the being already is.

4. The Argument from Will and Aseity

If the necessary being is the source of contingent existence, and contingent things did not *have* to exist, then their existence required some kind of selection among possibilities. Selection among possibilities is precisely what will does. A purely mechanical necessary cause would produce its effect necessarily, but then the contingent world would itself be necessary, which contradicts its contingency. Therefore something like *will*, a free orientation toward one possibility over others, seems required to account for contingent existence at all.

The Case AGAINST Intelligence and Will

1. The Simplicity Objection

This is the most serious internal objection. Intelligence involves a *knower* relating to a *known*, a distinction between subject and object, between the act of knowing and the content known. Will involves a *subject* oriented toward an *object* of desire or choice. But strict divine simplicity rules out all such internal distinctions. If the being is absolutely simple, there are no internal relations, no subject-object structure, no before-and-after of deliberation. Intelligence and will as we conceive them seem to require exactly the kind of complexity that simplicity forbids.

2. The Immutability Objection

Willing involves moving from a state of not-yet-decided to decided, or from wanting to acting. Knowing a contingent world involves knowing things that change. Both seem to require the necessary being to *change* in response to contingent events, which violates immutability. A being that cannot change cannot deliberate, respond, or decide in any temporal sense. Classical theologians worked hard on this (eternal knowledge of temporal things, timeless willing of contingent outcomes), but the tension is real.

3. Spinoza's Challenge

Spinoza accepted necessary existence but firmly rejected intelligence and will as attributes of the necessary being (Deus sive Natura, God or Nature). His argument: attributing will and intellect to God anthropomorphizes what is really an infinite, impersonal substance. Will implies preference, and preference implies the being lacks something it reaches toward, which contradicts infinity and aseity. The necessary being on Spinoza's account is not a mind; it is the infinite ground of all modes of existence, operating by necessity, not choice. This is a fully coherent position that accepts the earlier derived properties while firmly rejecting personhood.

4. The Hume-Kant Epistemic Objection

Even if intelligence and will are *consistent* with necessary existence, we may have no legitimate grounds for *inferring* them. Our only experience of intelligence and will is in finite, embodied, contingent beings. Projecting these properties onto a radically different kind of being, infinite, simple, atemporal, may be an illegitimate analogical leap. We simply do not know what intelligence or will would even *mean* for such an entity.

The Crucial Distinction: Analogical Predication

Classical theology's most sophisticated response to these tensions is the doctrine of analogical predication, developed by Aquinas and refined over centuries. The claim is not that God has intelligence and will in exactly the sense humans do (univocal predication), nor that the words mean something completely different (equivocal predication), but that they apply analogically, pointing to something real in the necessary being that is the infinite, simple source of what we call intelligence and will in creatures.

This is philosophically careful but carries a cost: the more we emphasize how different divine intelligence and will are from ours, the less confident we can be that we are talking about anything recognizable at all. The concept may be coherent without being informative.

The Deepest Tension

There is an unresolved structural problem at the core:

- The properties derived from necessity alone (simplicity, immutability, aseity) point toward an impersonal absolute, more like Spinoza's Natura or Neoplatonism's One than a personal God.
- The properties needed for religion to be coherent (intelligence, will, responsiveness, love) point toward a **personal being** capable of relationship.

These two portraits pull in opposite directions. The necessary being of pure metaphysics and the personal God of religious experience may not be the same concept, or if they are, holding them together requires philosophical work of the highest order, work that remains genuinely incomplete.

Conclusion

Intelligence and will are **not straightforwardly entailed** by necessary existence in the way that aseity, immutability, and simplicity are. They require additional premises, from perfection, from the ordered structure of contingency, from the need to account for *why* a particular world exists. These arguments have real force and have persuaded many careful philosophers. But they face equally serious objections rooted in the very properties, simplicity, immutability, that necessary existence does entail.

The honest verdict is this: **necessary existence is compatible with intelligence and will, and there are positive reasons to attribute them, but they are not**

logically compelled by necessity alone. The step from *necessary being* to *minded being* is the single most important and most contested move in all of natural theology, and it remains, after centuries of argument, genuinely open.

Question 4: Would such a being have reasons or purposes for creating contingent beings?

Question:

Would such a being have reasons or purposes for creating contingent beings?

METHODOLOGY, Motive analysis. Once intellect and will are established (Q. 3), the question of creation shifts from 'can it create?' to 'why would it?' This shifts the inquiry from metaphysics to teleology. The answer must respect divine simplicity (no acquired motives) while accounting for contingent reality. This sets up the entire problem of revelation: if creation is purposive, the purpose can, in principle, be communicated.

Claude Opus 4.7

This is perhaps the most difficult question in the entire sequence, because it pushes hardest against the properties we have already derived.

The Core Tension

The problem can be stated sharply at the outset. We have already established that a necessary being would be:

- **Infinite and unlimited**, lacking nothing
- **Immutable**, incapable of changing state

- **Simple**, without internal complexity or unfulfilled potentiality
- **Self-sufficient (aseity)**, dependent on nothing outside itself

But a *reason* or *purpose* for acting typically implies:

- a **goal** not yet achieved
- a **lack** to be filled
- a **before and after**, deliberation followed by action
- a **benefit** to be gained

Every one of these implications contradicts the derived properties of a necessary being. This is not a peripheral difficulty. It strikes at the very intelligibility of the necessary being as a creator.

The Possible Frameworks

1. It Could Not Have Reasons in the Ordinary Sense

This is the most logically rigorous position. A necessary being that lacks nothing, cannot change, and is absolutely self-sufficient simply has no *space* in its nature for reasons or purposes as we understand them. Reasons are for beings with unfulfilled goals. Purposes are for beings moving from potentiality to actuality. The necessary being is pure actuality, there is nowhere for it to go, nothing for it to gain.

On this view, asking *why* a necessary being creates is a category error, like asking what is north of the North Pole. The question assumes a framework of motivation that simply does not apply.

Spinoza drew exactly this conclusion: the necessary being (*Deus sive Natura*) does not act *for* anything. Contingent things flow from its nature the way theorems flow from axioms, necessarily, impersonally, without purpose.

There is no *why* in the intentional sense, only the inexorable expression of infinite nature.

---

2. Goodness as Self-Diffusive (The Classical Theist Answer)

Aquinas, drawing on Neoplatonism, offered the most developed alternative. The principle is: *bonum est diffusivum sui*, goodness is by nature self-communicating. The necessary being, being infinite and purely actual, just *is* goodness itself. And goodness, by its very nature, tends to share itself, not out of lack or need, but as an overflow of what it already fully is.

On this account:

- Creation is not motivated by need but by **superabundance**
- The necessary being does not *gain* anything by creating
- Contingent beings exist as participations in, or finite reflections of, the infinite goodness that the necessary being simply is
- The "reason" for creation is not a goal to be achieved but an expression of what the necessary being already is in full

This is elegant because it avoids the implication of lack or change. But it faces a challenge: if the self-diffusion of goodness is necessary to the being's nature, then creation would seem to be necessary too, which collapses the distinction between the necessary being and contingent things, and undermines the contingency of the world.

Aquinas's response was that creation flows from will, not nature, the necessary being freely chooses to communicate its goodness. But this reintroduces the problem of will and change: how does a timeless, immutable being freely choose?

---

3. Freedom Without Deliberation

One sophisticated move is to distinguish between:

- **Deliberative freedom**, choosing after weighing alternatives over time
- **Libertarian timeless freedom**, a will that is fully determined by nothing external, whose act is eternal and simple, not preceded by deliberation

On this view, the necessary being's will is not an event in time but an eternal, simple act that timelessly "selects" a contingent world. There is no before-and-after, no deliberation, no change, just an eternal volitional fact that is part of what the necessary being simply is.

This preserves both immutability and freedom, but the cost is that "freedom" and "choice" here mean something so different from our experience of them that it is unclear how informative the claim is. A timeless, simple, eternal "choice" that never deliberates, never changes, and never could have been otherwise in any experiential sense strains the ordinary meaning of those words severely.

---

4. Love as a Possible Reason

Some philosophers and theologians argue that love, specifically the kind that gives without expectation of return, provides a reason for creation that does not imply lack. The necessary being, on this account, creates not to fulfill itself but to give existence and goodness to others for their own sake.

This is the most personally resonant answer, and it connects creation to something recognizable in human experience. But it faces a fundamental logical problem: **love implies a relation between lover and beloved**. If the beloved (contingent beings) does not yet exist, there is nothing to love. The necessary being cannot love creatures *into* existence, because the love presupposes what it is meant to explain. And if it loves the *idea* of creatures, we are back to internal complexity within a supposedly simple being.

Furthermore, love in any rich sense implies responsiveness, being affected by the state of the beloved. But a strictly immutable being cannot be affected by anything.

---

5. No Reason Was Needed, Existence Is Simply Given

A more deflationary answer rejects the framing entirely. The question "why did the necessary being create?" assumes creation required justification or motivation. But perhaps existence is simply given, the necessary being is, contingent things are, and seeking a further reason behind this is a demand that reality need not satisfy.

This echoes Wittgenstein's remark that explanation must come to an end somewhere, and Leibniz's question "why is there something rather than nothing?" may simply not have an answer that fits our ordinary notion of reasons and purposes. The existence of contingent beings may be a brute fact at the level of the necessary being's nature, not arbitrary, but not purposive in any sense we can unpack.

Question 4: Would such a being have reasons or purposes for creating contingent beings?

What Follows From Each Position

Framework	Implication
No reasons (Spinoza)	Creation is necessary, impersonal, purposeless, religion as relationship becomes incoherent
Self-diffusion of goodness	Creation is a free overflow, contingent beings reflect divine goodness but are not needed
Timeless freedom	Creation is freely willed but in a sense of "freedom" almost unrecognizable to us
Love	Richest religious meaning, but faces the sharpest logical difficulties
No reason needed	Honest but philosophically unsatisfying, stops inquiry rather than answering it

The Structural Problem Underneath All of This

Every framework above runs into the same underlying difficulty, which can be stated as a trilemma:

1. If the necessary being **had to** create, creation was necessary to its nature, then contingent beings are not truly contingent, and the necessary being is not truly self-sufficient.
2. If the necessary being **freely chose** to create, in any robust sense of free choice, then it underwent some kind of change or deliberation, violating immutability and simplicity.
3. If the necessary being **had no reason** to create, creation was random or purposeless, then the

structured, intelligible contingent world becomes inexplicable, and the necessary being seems less than fully rational.

None of these options is without serious cost. Classical theology has attempted to navigate between them for centuries, but the navigation requires increasingly technical and stipulative uses of words like "reason," "will," "freedom," and "love" that may ultimately obscure more than they illuminate.

Conclusion

A necessary being, as derived from the logic of non-contingency, would face profound difficulty having reasons or purposes for creation in any sense we would ordinarily recognize. The properties that make it metaphysically ultimate, infinity, simplicity, immutability, aseity, are precisely the properties that make motivation, purpose, and reason deeply problematic.

The most defensible conclusion is this: if the necessary being creates at all, its "reason" cannot be need, benefit, or deliberate choice in any familiar sense. The closest coherent candidate is something like the classical notion of goodness overflowing by its own nature, but even this either collapses creation into necessity or requires a conception of timeless free will so remote from ordinary meaning that it becomes difficult to evaluate.

What this reveals is a fundamental divergence between the God of metaphysics and the God of religion. The necessary being, rigorously derived, is a austere, impersonal absolute. The God who creates for love, who purposes a world, who relates to creatures, that being requires not just logical derivation but a further step: either philosophical argument that genuine personhood is compatible with all the derived properties, or a willingness to revise some of those properties in light of what a creating, purposing God would have to be like. Neither path is without cost, and neither has been conclusively completed.

Question 5: If a non-contingent being created contingent beings, would it be possible for them to know anything about it?

Question:

If a non-contingent being created contingent beings, would it be possible for them to know anything about it?

· METHODOLOGY, Epistemic possibility. Granting purposive creation (Q. 4), we now ask whether the gap between creator and creature is traversable from the creature's side. This is the epistemological precondition for everything that follows. If knowledge is impossible in principle, revelation is impossible. The answer must rely on analogy: creatures cannot know the being as it is in itself, but can know it through its effects and self-disclosure. Frames Q. 6.

Claude Opus 4.7

This question shifts the inquiry from metaphysics to epistemology, and introduces a new set of difficulties, because the gap between a necessary being and contingent knowers is not merely large but may be categorically unbridgeable.

The Epistemic Situation of Contingent Beings

We need to be clear about what contingent knowers are working with. A contingent being:

- Exists within time, acquiring knowledge sequentially
- Knows through faculties shaped by its particular, limited nature
- Has cognitive access only to what its faculties can reach
- Cannot step outside its own perspective to check whether that perspective is adequate

The necessary being, by contrast, is atemporal, simple, infinite, and unlike anything within the contingent order. The question is whether a bridge across this gap is possible, and if so, what kind.

Five Possible Modes of Knowledge

1. A Posteriori Inference, Reasoning From Effects

The most philosophically modest route. Contingent beings observe the world around them and reason backward to its cause or ground. This is the method of the classical cosmological and teleological arguments, and it is the most defensible form of natural knowledge of a necessary being.

What it can establish:

- *That* something like a necessary being exists, as the explanation of contingent existence
- *Some* of its properties, power sufficient to ground contingent existence, some kind of ordering capacity, uniqueness

What it cannot establish:

- The *inner nature* of the necessary being, what it is like from the inside
- Whether it has intellect, will, or purpose in any meaningful sense
- Any specific intentions toward contingent beings

Question 5: If a non-contingent being created contingent beings, would it be possible for them to know anything about it?

The fundamental limitation is that effects underdetermine their causes. Many different causes could produce the same observed effect. Inferring the full nature of the necessary being from the contingent world is like trying to reconstruct a complete portrait from its shadow. The shadow tells you something real, but how much, and how accurately, is deeply uncertain.

---

2. A Priori Reasoning, Pure Conceptual Analysis

This is the route we have been taking throughout this conversation. Starting from the concept of necessary existence and deriving properties by logical entailment.

What it can establish:

- The structural properties of a necessary being, aseity, simplicity, immutability, uniqueness, and so on
- What a necessary being *cannot* be, composite, caused, temporal, limited

What it cannot establish:

- Whether such a being actually exists
- Anything about its concrete character beyond the logical skeleton
- Whether the concepts we use are genuinely adequate to the being, or merely the best approximations our finite minds can form

The limitation here is that conceptual analysis operates entirely within our conceptual scheme. We cannot be sure that our concepts, forged in experience of the contingent world, can reach all the way to something categorically beyond that world without distortion. We may be mapping our own cognitive limitations onto reality.

3. The Analogy Route, Knowing Through Resemblance

If contingent beings are in some sense *caused* by or *grounded in* the necessary being, they may resemble it in attenuated ways, the way an effect bears traces of its cause. This is the classical doctrine of **analogia entis**, the analogy of being, developed most fully by Aquinas.

The argument runs: when we say the necessary being is "good" or "intelligent," we are not using these words in exactly the sense we use them of creatures (univocal predication), nor in a completely different sense (equivocal predication), but analogically, pointing to something genuinely present in the necessary being of which creaturely goodness and intelligence are finite, imperfect participations.

What this allows:

- Genuine, if imperfect, cognitive contact with real properties of the necessary being
- A middle path between claiming full knowledge and claiming complete ignorance

The serious objection:

- The more we emphasize the difference between divine and creaturely properties, the thinner the analogy becomes
- At the limit, "God is good" in such a radically different sense from "humans are good" that it becomes unclear whether the sentence carries real information
- Analogy may tell us the necessary being is *the source* of what we call goodness without telling us what goodness *is* in that being

4. The Via Negativa, Knowing by Negation

An influential tradition, prominent in Maimonides, Pseudo-Dionysius, and Plotinus, argues that the only reliable knowledge of a necessary being is *negative*: knowing what it is *not* rather than what it is.

We can reliably say:

- It is not contingent
- It is not composite
- It is not temporal
- It is not limited
- It is not caused

This is epistemically modest but genuinely informative. Stripping away every contingent, finite, composite property still leaves a kind of cognitive achievement, we are progressively isolating something by ruling out what cannot apply to it.

The limitation is obvious: negative knowledge alone never tells us what something positively *is*. We may successfully clear the ground without ever building anything on it. A being defined entirely by negations remains, from our perspective, essentially unknown in its positive nature.

5. Direct Disclosure, Revelation

If the necessary being has intellect and will, which we established is possible but not certain, then it could in principle *choose* to make itself known to contingent beings in ways that go beyond what they could discover on their own. This is the concept of **revelation** in religious traditions.

Philosophically, this is not incoherent. If a necessary being exists and is minded, self-disclosure is within the logical space of what it could do. The question is entirely one of *evidence*: how would contingent beings distinguish genuine disclosure from illusion, misinterpretation, or projection?

This is where philosophy reaches its natural limit and hands the question to history, testimony, and the evaluation of specific religious claims, which cannot be settled by metaphysical reasoning alone. Philosophy can establish that revelation is *possible*; it cannot establish that any particular revelation *occurred*.

The Fundamental Epistemic Barrier

Underlying all five routes is a single deep problem: **the necessary being, if our derivations are correct, is categorically unlike anything contingent knowers have direct access to.**

Consider the asymmetry:

- We know contingent things by encountering them, through perception, interaction, causal contact
- The necessary being is not an object within the contingent order to be encountered
- It is the *ground* of the contingent order, which means it is related to experience the way a canvas is related to a painting, not the way one object in the painting is related to another

This means our normal epistemic machinery, perception, induction, scientific method, is not calibrated for this kind of object. We are using instruments designed for contingent reality to try to detect what lies beyond contingent reality. The instruments may give real readings, or they may simply be registering their own limitations.

Kant made this point with great force: our cognitive faculties are structured for experience of the phenomenal world. When we try to apply them beyond that world, to things in themselves, to the unconditioned ground of experience, we inevitably fall into antinomies and illusions. The necessary being, on Kant's account, is a regulative idea, useful for organizing inquiry, but not a possible object of knowledge in the strict sense.

What Contingent Beings Could Reasonably Claim to Know

Pulling the threads together, there is a spectrum from more to less epistemically secure:

More secure:

- That *something* functions as the necessary ground of contingent existence
- What the necessary being is *not*, the via negativa results
- The structural-logical properties derived by a priori reasoning, uniqueness, aseity, simplicity, and so on
- That knowledge of it, if possible at all, must be radically unlike knowledge of contingent things

Less secure:

- That it has intelligence and will in any meaningful sense
- That it has purposes or intentions regarding contingent beings
- That analogical language about goodness, love, or wisdom genuinely reaches it

Beyond what unaided reason can establish:

- Anything about its specific intentions, character, or relation to particular contingent beings
- Whether it has disclosed itself in history or experience
- Whether any religious tradition accurately represents it

Conclusion

Contingent beings could know *something* about a necessary being, but the knowledge is structurally limited in ways that cannot be overcome by greater effort or cleverness. The limits are not incidental but follow from the categorical difference between a necessary being and everything that contingent knowers are and have access to.

The most honest summary is this: **contingent beings could know that a necessary being exists, and could derive its formal properties, but would face an increasingly steep epistemic gradient the more they tried to know about its inner nature, its purposes, or its relation to them specifically.** Natural reason reaches a genuine but narrow ledge, enough to establish that something of enormous metaphysical significance exists, not enough to know it in the way religious traditions typically claim.

Whether that ledge can be extended, by revelation, by mystical experience, by some cognitive mode not yet accounted for, is a question that rigorous philosophy can pose but cannot, by its own methods, answer. That may itself be the most important conclusion of the entire inquiry: the necessary being, if it exists, is precisely the kind of thing that would permanently exceed the grasp of the contingent minds it grounds, and that asymmetry is not a failure of philosophy but one of its deepest results.

Question 6: Would it be more rational for such knowledge to come through self-discovery, external communication, or both?

Question:

Would it be more rational for such knowledge to come through self-discovery, external communication, or both?

METHODOLOGY, Mode of knowing. Given that knowledge is possible (Q. 5), what is its rational form? This question distinguishes natural theology (self-discovery from creation) from revealed theology (external communication). The 'both' answer is structurally important: it preserves human reason while requiring revelation for what reason cannot reach unaided. It sets up Q. 7 by asking whether the communicating side has reason to initiate.

Claude Opus 4.7

This question is really asking about the *optimal epistemic structure* for knowledge of a necessary being, which is a fascinating question because the answer is not obvious, and depends on assumptions that themselves require examination.

Question 6: Would it be more rational for such knowledge to come through self-discovery, external communication, or both?

Clarifying the Options

Self-discovery means contingent beings arriving at knowledge of the necessary being through their own cognitive resources, reason, observation, inference, introspection, mystical experience. The knower is active; the necessary being is passive with respect to the knowing.

External communication means the necessary being actively disclosing itself, conveying information that contingent beings could not have reached, or could not have reached reliably, on their own. The necessary being is active; the knower receives.

Both means some combination, perhaps self-discovery establishes a foundation that makes communication intelligible, or communication corrects and extends what self-discovery partially achieves.

The Case for Self-Discovery Alone

Epistemic Autonomy

Knowledge arrived at through one's own reasoning carries a kind of warrant that received knowledge does not. You can examine the steps, test the conclusions, identify weak premises. Self-discovered knowledge is, in principle, fully transparent to the knower, you know not just that something is true but why it is true. This is the Enlightenment ideal: reason answerable to nothing but itself.

No Authentication Problem

External communication immediately raises the question: how do contingent beings know the communication is genuine? Any purported disclosure from a necessary being arrives through contingent channels, human testimony, texts, experiences, traditions, all of which are fallible, interpretable, and susceptible to distortion. Self-discovery bypasses this problem entirely. The argument either holds or it does not; there is no middleman to distrust.

Consistency With the Necessary Being's Nature

A necessary being that is immutable and atemporal may not be capable of *communicating* in any straightforward sense, communication implies an event in time, a change in the epistemic state of the receiver caused by an act of the sender. If the necessary being cannot act in time without compromising its immutability, then external communication may be metaphysically unavailable. Self-discovery would then not merely be preferable but necessary.

The Serious Limitation

We already established in the previous exchange that self-discovery has a hard ceiling. The necessary being is categorically unlike anything within the contingent order. Reason can establish that it exists and derive its formal properties, but cannot penetrate its inner nature, cannot determine whether it has purposes, and cannot know whether it has any specific relation to particular contingent beings. Self-discovery alone leaves the most religiously and existentially significant questions permanently unanswered.

The Case for External Communication Alone

This position is rarely held in its pure form, but its logic deserves examination. If the necessary being has intellect and will, and if it created contingent beings for some purpose, it would presumably have reason to ensure those beings could actually know what they need to know. If self-discovery is structurally insufficient, which the previous analysis strongly suggests, then external communication would be the only reliable path.

The Fatal Problem

External communication without any prior self-discovery creates an insurmountable authentication problem. To receive and evaluate a communication from a necessary being, contingent knowers need *some* prior framework, some concept of what a necessary being is, some capacity to distinguish genuine disclosure from false. A communication arriving into a completely unprepared mind would be uninterpretable. Pure external communication with no self-discovery would be epistemically inert, like sending a message in a language the recipient has no resources to begin decoding.

The Case for Both, and Why It Is More Rational

The combination is not merely a diplomatic compromise. There are strong structural reasons why both are required, and why they stand in a specific relationship to each other.

Self-Discovery as Necessary Precondition

Before external communication can be received, evaluated, or understood, contingent knowers need:

- The concept of a necessary being, so the communication has a referent
- Some grasp of its properties, so claims about it can be assessed for coherence
- Rational criteria for evaluating testimony and experience, so genuine disclosure can be distinguished from illusion or manipulation

Self-discovery provides exactly this foundation. Natural theology, the a priori and a posteriori reasoning we have been conducting, delivers a conceptual framework into which communication can arrive meaningfully. Without it, communication would be noise.

External Communication as Necessary Extension

But self-discovery, as we established, cannot penetrate the inner nature of the necessary being, cannot determine its purposes, and cannot establish its specific relation to contingent beings. If any of this is knowable at all, it must come from the necessary being's own initiative.

More precisely, there are three things self-discovery structurally cannot deliver:

Particular intentions. Even if we know the necessary being is the ground of contingent existence, we cannot know by reason alone whether it has specific purposes for specific beings or kinds of beings. Particularity exceeds what universal reasoning can reach.

Relational knowledge. Knowing about something and knowing it, in the sense of genuine mutual relation, are different. A necessary being that is purely an object of inference remains at arm's length. If genuine relation between the necessary being and contingent beings is possible, it likely requires some form of self-disclosure that makes relation, not just inference, available.

Correction of distortion. Self-discovery is conducted by finite, contingent minds using concepts forged in experience of the contingent world. There is no guarantee, and some reason to doubt, that these concepts apply cleanly to a necessary being. External communication could correct systematic distortions that self-discovery alone could not detect, precisely because you cannot see the limitations of your own conceptual scheme from inside it.

The Optimal Structure

If we take both as necessary, the rational structure of knowledge about a necessary being would look something like this:

First: Self-discovery establishes that a necessary being exists and derives its formal properties. This is the indispensable rational foundation, without it, nothing that follows can be evaluated.

Second: Self-discovery reaches its ceiling, recognizing its own limits is itself a product of rigorous inquiry. The honest conclusion of natural theology is not confident knowledge of the necessary being's full nature but awareness of how much remains unreachable.

Third: The question of external communication becomes genuinely open, not as a retreat from reason but as a rational response to reason's acknowledged limits. If the necessary being has will and purpose, self-disclosure is possible. Whether it has occurred is an empirical and historical question, not a purely philosophical one.

Fourth: Any purported external communication must be evaluated against the framework established by self-discovery. Communications that contradict the derived properties of a necessary being, claiming it is composite, contingent, limited, or multiple, can be rationally assessed as suspect. Self-discovery provides the criteria by which communication is evaluated.

Fifth: Communication, if genuine, would extend rather than replace self-discovery, filling in what reason left open rather than contradicting what reason established. The two modes would be complementary, not competitive.

A Deeper Point, The Problem of Recognition

There is a subtle but important issue that the combination resolves in a way neither alone can.

For external communication to be received as such, as genuine disclosure from a necessary being rather than a contingent event misinterpreted, the recipient must already have some sense of what a necessary being is. Otherwise they cannot recognize the communication as coming from *it* rather than from something else.

But for self-discovery to motivate continued inquiry and openness to communication, the knower must already suspect that reason alone is insufficient, that there is more to know than inference can reach.

Each mode thus *prepares the ground for the other.* Self-discovery creates the conceptual space into which communication can arrive meaningfully. The limits of self-discovery create the rational openness that makes the possibility of communication worth taking seriously rather than dismissing. This mutual preparation is not accidental, it suggests that the two modes are not merely compatible but structurally designed for each other, at least if the necessary being is the kind of being that both grounds contingent existence and has intentions toward contingent knowers.

The Rationality Verdict

The question was which route is *more rational,* and the answer, carefully considered, is that rationality itself favors the combination, for the following reasons:

A rational knower:

Question 6: Would it be more rational for such knowledge to come through self-discovery, external communication, or both?

- Uses all available and legitimate epistemic routes rather than arbitrarily restricting inquiry
- Recognizes the limits of each method honestly
- Does not mistake the absence of self-discovered knowledge for proof of absence
- Remains open to evidence from sources beyond those already consulted, provided that evidence can be evaluated by reliable criteria
- Does not accept communication uncritically, but evaluates it against independently established standards

All of these commitments point toward a combination in which self-discovery does the foundational and evaluative work, and genuine openness to communication fills what self-discovery cannot reach.

Conclusion

Neither self-discovery alone nor external communication alone is fully rational as an exclusive strategy. Self-discovery alone is rationally admirable but hits a structural ceiling it cannot overcome by its own resources. External communication alone is epistemically helpless without a rational framework to receive and evaluate it.

The most rational position is a structured combination in which **self-discovery is primary and foundational, establishing what can be known and, crucially, what cannot, and external communication is recognized as the only possible source of what self-discovery leaves open, to be evaluated critically against the framework self-discovery provides.**

This conclusion has a striking implication: the person who reasons most carefully about a necessary being, who follows the logic most rigorously to its limits, is not thereby driven away from the possibility of revelation, but is arguably better positioned to evaluate it than someone who either uncritically accepts it or dismisses it without inquiry. Rigorous natural theology and genuine openness to disclosure are not opposites. They may be, in the end, two phases of a single rational project.

Question 7: Would an intelligent non-contingent being have reasons to communicate with contingent beings?

Question:

Would an intelligent non-contingent being have reasons to communicate with contingent beings?

METHODOLOGY, Reciprocity. Q. 6 established that contingent beings could rationally receive communication. This question asks the symmetric one: would the non-contingent being have reason to send it? The answer must derive from the properties already established (goodness, intellect, purposive will). If yes, revelation is not just possible but expected, which raises the burden of finding it.

Claude Opus 4.7

This question presses directly on one of the most consequential joints in the entire argument, because if the answer is yes, it transforms the necessary being from a metaphysical abstraction into something with genuine orientation toward contingent knowers, which has enormous implications.

The Difficulty Restated

We must hold two things in tension simultaneously. On one side, we have derived that the necessary being is infinite, simple, immutable, and self-sufficient, lacking nothing, needing nothing, incapable of being improved or diminished by anything outside itself. On the other side, the question asks whether such a being could have *reasons*, which implies goals, orientations, and purposes directed outward.

The tension is real. A being that lacks nothing appears to have no grounds for any outward orientation whatsoever. And yet, if it has intelligence and will, which we established is possible, then pure inward closure seems equally difficult to maintain. An intelligent being with no orientation toward anything is a strange concept. Intelligence without any object is arguably not intelligence at all.

Possible Reasons to Communicate

1. Communication as Expression of Goodness

We already encountered the classical principle that goodness is self-diffusive, *bonum est diffusivum sui*. If the necessary being simply *is* goodness in its fullness, and if communication is a form of self-sharing, then communicating with contingent beings would be a natural expression of what the necessary being already is.

Crucially, this reason does not imply need or lack. The necessary being does not communicate *in order to* become good, or *in order to* fulfill itself. It communicates as an overflow of what it already fully is, the way light illuminates not because it needs to but because illumination is simply what light does.

This is the most metaphysically careful positive answer available. It grounds communication in the necessary being's nature rather than in any external goal, thereby avoiding the implication of deficiency.

The objection remains: if communication is necessary to the nature of goodness, then the necessary being would *have* to communicate, which compromises its freedom and potentially its aseity. If communication is not necessary but merely possible, we still need an account of what tips the balance toward actually communicating rather than not.

---

2. Communication as Completion of the Creative Act

If the necessary being created contingent beings at all, which is itself not logically compelled but possible, then communication might follow as the natural completion of that act. Creating beings capable of intelligence and then withholding all knowledge of their ground and source would be, at minimum, a strange truncation of the creative intention.

Put differently: if contingent beings were created with cognitive faculties oriented toward truth, and if the most fundamental truth is the existence and nature of the necessary being, then creating such beings without providing any means of knowing that truth would be a kind of internal incoherence in the creative act itself. Communication would not be a separate decision but the fulfillment of what creation already implied.

This argument has real force, but it is conditional on two things we cannot establish by reason alone, that the necessary being created intentionally, and that it created beings with cognitive faculties for a purpose. If creation was purposeless or necessary rather than free, this argument dissolves.

---

3. Communication as the Basis for Genuine Relation

If the necessary being is in any sense personal, possessing intelligence and will, then the question arises whether it can stand in genuine relation to contingent beings. Relation requires mutuality: both parties must in some sense be present to each other.

But contingent beings, left entirely to self-discovery, relate to the necessary being only as an inferred conclusion, an object of reasoning, not a subject of encounter. This is a profoundly asymmetric and attenuated form of relation. For genuine relation to be possible, whatever that would mean between a necessary and a contingent being, some form of self-disclosure by the necessary being seems required. Communication would be the condition of possibility for relation, not merely one of its expressions.

If the necessary being has any orientation toward relation with contingent beings, and a personal being with no relational orientation is arguably a diminished form of personhood, then it would have reason to communicate precisely in order to make relation possible.

---

4. Communication as Correction of Inevitable Distortion

We established in the previous exchange that self-discovery, conducted by finite minds using contingent concepts, will inevitably involve distortion. Contingent knowers cannot step outside their own cognitive limitations to check whether their conception of the necessary being is adequate. They are, epistemically speaking, in a closed room trying to describe what lies outside.

An intelligent necessary being, observing this predicament, would have reason to communicate simply to prevent its contingent knowers from systematically mistaking what it is. If the necessary being has any interest in being known accurately, which an intelligent being plausibly would, then communication is the only available corrective to the distortion that self-discovery alone will inevitably produce.

This is a relatively modest but sturdy argument. It does not require strong claims about the necessary being's love or purpose, only that an intelligent being would prefer accurate understanding to systematic misrepresentation, and would act on that preference if it could.

5. Communication as Enabling the Good of Contingent Beings

If contingent beings are better off knowing the necessary being than not knowing it, which is plausible if it is genuinely the ground of their existence and the source of whatever goodness they possess, then an intelligent necessary being with any orientation toward the good of its creatures would have reason to communicate.

This argument connects to classical accounts of *beatitude* or *flourishing*, the idea that contingent rational beings have a natural orientation toward the necessary being as their ultimate end, and that their deepest fulfillment consists in some form of knowledge of or union with it. If this is correct, withholding communication would be withholding the very thing contingent beings most fundamentally need, which an intelligent, good necessary being would have strong reason not to do.

The objection is that this imports a thick ethical framework, that the necessary being *cares* about the flourishing of contingent beings, which is not straightforwardly derived from necessity alone. It depends on the necessary being being not merely intelligent but benevolent in an outward-directed sense.

Reasons Against Communication

1. Perfect Self-Sufficiency Leaves No Motivational Room

The most serious objection is the one with which we began. A being that is infinite, immutable, and self-sufficient has, in the strictest sense, nothing to gain from communication. Every reason we have considered, expressing goodness, completing creation, enabling relation, correcting distortion, promoting flourishing, is ultimately a reason from the perspective of contingent beings, not from the perspective of the necessary being itself.

From within the necessary being's nature, as we have derived it, there is simply no unfulfilled orientation, no unrealized potential, no gap that communication fills. This is not a criticism of the necessary being, it follows from its perfection. But it means that the reasons we have been considering are really reasons we can see from the outside, not motivations that arise from within the necessary being's nature.

2. Communication Implies Temporal Action

Any act of communication is an event, it occurs at a time, produces a change in the receiver, and involves the sender in a relation that did not previously obtain. All of this sits uncomfortably with immutability and atemporality. If the necessary being cannot act in time without compromising its derived properties, then communication in any ordinary sense may be metaphysically unavailable to it, regardless of whether it has reasons for it.

The standard response, that the necessary being's communicative act is eternal and simple, producing temporal effects without itself being temporal, is coherent but again requires "communication" to mean something very different from what we ordinarily understand.

3. The Incomprehensibility Barrier

Even if the necessary being had reasons to communicate and the metaphysical capacity to do so, there is a question of whether communication could succeed. The necessary being, as derived, is so categorically unlike anything in the contingent order that any communication would require radical translation into contingent terms, terms that inevitably distort what they attempt to convey.

This is not merely a practical difficulty. It may be a principled barrier: the necessary being cannot communicate what it is in terms that contingent minds can fully receive, because contingent minds are precisely the kind of thing that cannot contain that content. Communication might therefore be possible only in a permanently partial, analogical, and potentially misleading form, which raises the question of whether such communication is better than the silence of self-discovery.

The Asymmetry That Matters Most

There is a fundamental asymmetry in this question that deserves emphasis. From the perspective of contingent beings, the reasons for the necessary being to communicate are enormous, it would address their deepest epistemic limitations, provide the knowledge most relevant to their existence, and enable a form of relation they cannot initiate themselves.

From the perspective of the necessary being, insofar as we can speak of such a perspective, the reasons are internal to its nature and properties, and require the attribution of outward orientation that is not straightforwardly derived from necessity alone.

This asymmetry suggests something important: the question of whether the necessary being has reasons to communicate cannot be settled from the outside. Contingent beings can see why communication would matter enormously to them. They cannot, by their own reasoning, determine whether the necessary being's nature includes the kind of outward orientation that would make communication a live possibility for it.

This is precisely the point at which self-discovery reaches its most fundamental limit, not merely a limit of information, but a limit of perspective. The necessary being's reasons, if it has them, are interior to a nature that contingent reasoning cannot fully penetrate.

Conclusion

An intelligent necessary being would have several genuine candidate reasons to communicate with contingent beings, the self-diffusive nature of goodness, the completion of creative intent, the enabling of genuine relation, the correction of inevitable epistemic distortion, and the promotion of contingent flourishing. None of these reasons implies need or lack in the necessary being; the strongest of them flow from what the necessary being already is rather than from any external goal.

However, the honest conclusion must acknowledge three limits. First, these reasons depend on attributing to the necessary being properties, particularly outward-directed goodness and relational orientation, that are possible but not strictly entailed by necessary existence alone. Second, the metaphysical difficulties around communication, its apparent incompatibility with strict immutability and atemporality, remain unresolved. Third, and most deeply, the necessary being's own perspective on these reasons is precisely what contingent reasoning cannot access.

What we can say with confidence is this: **if the necessary being is intelligent, and if it created contingent beings with cognitive faculties oriented toward truth, then the reasons for communication are not merely sentimental but follow from the internal logic of what intelligence, goodness, and creation already imply.** A necessary being that created rational knowers and then remained entirely silent would be, at minimum, internally inconsistent, creating beings structured for a knowledge it then made permanently unavailable.

That argument does not prove communication occurred. But it establishes something philosophically significant: communication would not be an arbitrary or inexplicable act on the necessary being's part. It would be the rational completion of a trajectory already implicit in the act of creating intelligent contingent beings at all. The question of whether it actually happened is one that reason can pose with full seriousness, but can only begin to answer by looking outward, into history and experience, rather than inward, into the logic of necessary existence alone.

Question 8: If communication occurred, would it be more rational for it to be orderly or chaotic?

Question:

If communication occurred, would it be more rational for it to be orderly or chaotic?

METHODOLOGY, the formal structure of revelation. Granting that communication would occur (Q. 7), what shape would it take? This is a question about form, not content. An orderly communication reflects the orderliness of the communicator (Q. 2 properties: simplicity, unity). A chaotic revelation would be self-undermining; it would falsify the very attributes that motivated it. This sets the criterion against which historical religions will be measured.

Claude Opus 4.7

This question appears simple at first but opens into a rich set of considerations, because the answer, while ultimately clear, requires careful argument to establish properly rather than being assumed from the outset.

What Orderly and Chaotic Communication Would Mean

Before evaluating which is more rational, we need to be precise about what these terms mean in this context.

Orderly communication would be coherent, consistent, intelligible, purposive, and structured in ways that contingent minds can progressively engage with. It would hang together internally, avoid contradiction, and be suited to the cognitive capacities of its recipients.

Chaotic communication would be random, contradictory, unintelligible, without discernible structure or purpose, varying arbitrarily, and bearing no reliable relationship between its form and any intended content.

The Case for Orderly Communication

1. It Follows Directly From the Nature of the Necessary Being

We have derived that the necessary being is simple, unified, immutable, and the ground of all contingent order. A being that is the source of whatever structure, regularity, and intelligibility exists in the contingent world would not produce communication that contradicts its own nature. Chaos is the absence of order, and the necessary being, as the ground of order, cannot be the source of its own negation without internal contradiction.

This is perhaps the strongest argument, because it does not require attributing any additional properties to the necessary being beyond those already derived. Orderly communication follows analytically from what the necessary being already is.

2. Chaotic Communication Would Defeat Its Own Purpose

We established in the previous exchange that the necessary being would have reasons to communicate, correcting distortion, enabling relation, completing the creative act, promoting flourishing. Every one of these reasons presupposes that the communication *succeeds*, that it actually conveys something, reaches the recipient in a form they can engage with, and produces accurate rather than distorted understanding.

Chaotic communication achieves none of these goals. A communication that is random, contradictory, or unintelligible does not correct distortion, it compounds it. It does not enable relation, it prevents it. It does not promote flourishing, it produces confusion. Chaotic communication is self-defeating with respect to every reason we identified for communicating at all.

A rational being does not adopt means that undermine its own ends. Therefore an intelligent necessary being, communicating for any of the reasons we identified, would communicate in an orderly way.

3. The Capacities of the Recipients Determine the Form

Communication is always calibrated to its recipients. A message perfectly formed in one medium is useless if delivered in a medium the recipient cannot process. Contingent rational beings have specific cognitive structures, they reason sequentially, identify patterns, evaluate coherence, and build understanding cumulatively. These capacities are themselves ordered, they are structured for engagement with intelligible content.

Chaotic communication would be systematically mismatched to the cognitive architecture of contingent rational knowers. It would not merely be difficult to understand, it would be, in principle, unrecognizable as communication at all. Random noise cannot be distinguished from meaningful signal without some structure to identify it as the latter. An intelligent necessary being aware of its recipients' cognitive structure would therefore not produce communication they are constitutionally unable to receive.

4. Order Is a Condition of Recognizability

This point deserves particular emphasis. For contingent beings to recognize something as *communication from a necessary being* rather than as a natural event, coincidence, or psychological projection, the communication must exhibit properties that distinguish it from background noise. Order, coherence, and intelligibility are precisely what make communication recognizable as such.

A necessary being that communicated chaotically would produce something indistinguishable from no communication at all, which would defeat the purpose entirely. Orderliness is not merely a desirable feature of communication but a condition of its being identifiable as communication in the first place.

5. Truth Is Ordered

If the necessary being communicates, it presumably communicates truly, a being that is the ground of reality communicating falsehoods would be internally incoherent. But truth itself has structure. Truths cohere with each other, exclude their contradictions, and form an intelligible whole. Communication of truth therefore cannot be chaotic, because chaos is incompatible with the coherent structure of what is true. The form of the communication must reflect the ordered character of its content.

The Case for Chaotic Communication, Steelmanned

It would be intellectually dishonest not to consider whether there are any serious reasons to expect chaotic communication. There are a few candidates, though none ultimately succeeds.

1. The Incomprehensibility of the Necessary Being

We have repeatedly acknowledged that the necessary being is categorically beyond full comprehension by contingent minds. Perhaps chaotic communication, resistant to systematic understanding, better reflects the genuine incomprehensibility of its source than orderly communication, which might create a false impression of full comprehension.

This is a real insight but does not support chaotic communication. The appropriate response to genuine incomprehensibility is not chaos but *acknowledged limit*, orderly communication that clearly marks where understanding runs out. A map that clearly shows the edge of explored territory is more honest than random scribbling. Chaos does not convey incomprehensibility, it merely conveys noise.

2. Freedom and Unpredictability

If the necessary being has genuine will and freedom, perhaps its communication would be irreducibly spontaneous, not subject to any pattern that contingent minds could anticipate. Radical freedom might manifest as apparent chaos.

But this confuses unpredictability with incoherence. A free being can act in ways that are not mechanically predictable while still acting consistently, purposively, and intelligibly. Human freedom does not produce random noise, it produces coherent but non-determined action. Freedom and order are not opposites. The necessary being's freedom would be expressed in what it chooses to communicate, not in communicating in a way that defeats comprehension.

3. Testing or Developing Contingent Knowers

Perhaps chaotic communication serves a pedagogical function, forcing contingent knowers to develop greater cognitive and interpretive capacities by presenting them with material that resists easy comprehension.

This is the most interesting of the three candidates. There is something genuinely plausible about the idea that the best communication is not the easiest but the most growth-producing. However, even this argument does not support genuine chaos, it supports *difficulty*, *depth*, and *inexhaustibility*, which are entirely compatible with order. The most demanding texts, the most complex mathematics, the most profound music, all are deeply ordered while remaining difficult and generative. Chaos does not challenge; it merely defeats.

A Crucial Distinction: Order vs. Simplicity

Establishing that communication would be orderly does not mean it would be simple, immediately transparent, or exhaustively comprehensible. These are different properties and the argument here does not establish them.

Orderly communication from a necessary being might be:

- **Inexhaustibly deep**, yielding new understanding at every level of engagement without ever being fully exhausted

- **Progressively intelligible**, requiring sustained engagement rather than immediate comprehension
- **Analogical rather than literal**, structured and coherent, but pointing beyond itself to what cannot be directly expressed
- **Layered**, carrying meaning at multiple levels simultaneously, each ordered but none complete

All of these are compatible with order while explaining why genuine communication from a necessary being would remain permanently demanding and partially opaque. The order would be real; the full comprehension would remain asymptotically approachable but never achieved.

This distinction matters because it prevents a naive reading of the conclusion. Orderly communication from a necessary being would not be a simple, clear manual fully comprehensible to any reader. It would be communication that *rewards* ordered engagement, coherent enough to be progressively understood, deep enough never to be fully exhausted.

The Meta-Point: Rationality Itself Presupposes Order

There is a final argument that underlies all the others and is worth making explicit. The question asks what is *more rational*, and rationality itself is a form of order. To reason about this question at all, we are already committed to the value and reliability of ordered thought.

A necessary being that communicated chaotically would be undermining the very cognitive capacity by which its contingent knowers could receive, evaluate, and respond to communication. It would be simultaneously appealing to reason and destroying the grounds of reason. This is not merely impractical, it is self-contradictory. Chaotic communication from an intelligent necessary being would be the cognitive equivalent of creating rational beings and then making rationality unreliable, an act that defeats itself completely.

Conclusion

The answer here is one of the clearest in the entire sequence of questions. It would be overwhelmingly more rational for communication from an intelligent necessary being to be orderly rather than chaotic, for reasons that converge from every direction:

It follows from the necessary being's own nature as the ground of order. It is required by the internal logic of having reasons to communicate at all. It is demanded by the cognitive structure of the contingent beings who are the recipients. It is a condition of the communication being recognizable as such. It is entailed by the ordered character of truth itself. And chaotic communication would be self-defeating with respect to every purpose that could motivate communication in the first place.

The more interesting and genuinely open question is not whether communication would be orderly but *what kind* of order it would exhibit, whether linear or cumulative, whether propositional or experiential, whether addressed to individuals or communities or both, whether delivered once or progressively over time. These questions take us beyond what pure reasoning can determine. But on the fundamental question of order versus chaos, the logic points in one direction without serious ambiguity.

Question 8: If communication occurred, would it be more rational for it to be orderly or chaotic?

An intelligent necessary being that communicated chaotically would be contradicting its own nature, defeating its own purposes, and destroying the very cognitive capacity it was attempting to address. Orderly communication is not merely preferable, it is the only form consistent with what we have established the necessary being to be.

Question 9: Would a structured communication system be expected to have continuity over time?

Question:

Would a structured communication system be expected to have continuity over time?

METHODOLOGY, Temporal persistence. Order (Q. 8) must persist or it is not order at all, it is a momentary event. This question introduces history as a test variable. A revelation that fails to continue is indistinguishable from a non-revelation after one generation. This is the criterion that begins to filter out movements, sects, and ruptures. Prepares for Q. 10 (mechanism of continuity).

Claude Opus 4.7

This question moves the inquiry into territory with increasingly concrete implications, because continuity over time is not merely a desirable feature of communication but, as we will see, something close to a logical requirement given everything already established.

What Continuity Would Mean Here

Continuity over time in a structured communication system would mean at minimum:

- **Persistence**, the communication is not a single isolated event but endures and remains accessible
- **Consistency**, later communications do not contradict earlier ones without explanation
- **Coherence**, the system develops as a unified whole rather than fragmenting into unrelated pieces
- **Cumulativeness**, understanding builds progressively, with later communications deepening rather than erasing earlier ones
- **Identifiability**, the system remains recognizable as coming from the same source across time

The question is whether these properties are rationally expected, merely possible, or unnecessary.

The Case for Continuity

1. It Follows From the Nature of the Source

The necessary being is immutable and simple. Its nature does not change, its truth does not evolve, and its purposes, if it has them, do not shift arbitrarily. A communication system originating from such a source would be expected to reflect that stability. Discontinuity in the communication, radical breaks, reversals, contradictions without resolution, would suggest either multiple sources or an inconsistent source. Neither is compatible with what we have derived.

This is the most fundamental argument. The communication system is, in a sense, a temporal expression of an atemporal reality. Just as the contingent world exhibits regular, lawlike behavior because it is grounded in a necessary being that does not change, a communication system from that being would be expected to exhibit analogous regularity and consistency across time.

2. Contingent Recipients Exist in Time

The necessary being's communication is addressed to beings who are irreducibly temporal. They are born, develop, learn cumulatively, exist within communities that transmit knowledge across generations, and build understanding progressively rather than instantaneously. A communication system perfectly matched to such recipients would be structured for temporal engagement, not delivered all at once to a timeless mind, but sustained across time in forms that successive generations can access, appropriate, and transmit.

Continuity is therefore not merely a feature of the communication system in isolation but a requirement imposed by the nature of its recipients. A system that appeared once and then vanished would be accessible only to those present at that moment, which would arbitrarily privilege one generation of contingent beings over all others. Continuity is what makes the communication available across the full temporal extent of the contingent beings it is addressed to.

3. Understanding Develops Cumulatively

We established that orderly communication from a necessary being would be inexhaustibly deep, not fully comprehensible at first encounter but yielding progressive understanding through sustained engagement. This developmental character of understanding requires time. Insights build on each other; earlier communications create the conceptual framework within which later ones can be received; questions raised at one stage are addressed at another.

A communication system that lacked continuity, that appeared in disconnected episodes with no thread connecting them, would prevent exactly this kind of cumulative development. Each generation would begin from zero, unable to inherit and build on the understanding of previous generations. The depth that orderly communication from a necessary being would exhibit requires continuity as its condition of possibility.

4. Continuity Is Required for Authentication

We noted in the previous discussion that any purported communication from a necessary being faces an authentication problem, how do contingent beings know it is genuine? One of the most important criteria for evaluating this question is internal consistency across time. A communication system that maintains coherence over centuries or millennia, developing without contradiction, addressing new questions while remaining faithful to earlier commitments, provides evidence of a unified source that disconnected episodes cannot provide.

Continuity is therefore not merely useful for recipients but is part of what makes the communication system identifiable as coming from a single, consistent source, which is itself a criterion of its potential authenticity.

5. The Communicative Purpose Extends Across Time

The reasons we identified for the necessary being to communicate, correcting distortion, enabling relation, promoting the flourishing of contingent beings, are not reasons that apply only to one moment. Contingent beings exist across time; new ones come into existence continuously. If the necessary being's communicative purposes are genuine, they apply to contingent beings as such, not merely to those present at one particular moment.

This means the communication system must persist to serve its purpose. A communication addressed only to one generation and inaccessible to subsequent ones would achieve its purpose for a fraction of its intended audience while failing the rest, which would be internally inconsistent with the universality that the necessary being's nature implies.

What Kind of Continuity Would Be Expected

Establishing that continuity is rationally expected leaves open important questions about its character. Not all forms of continuity are equally rational given what we have established.

Progressive Rather Than Static

Continuity does not mean simple repetition of identical content. Given that contingent recipients develop cumulatively and that the communication system is inexhaustibly deep, continuity would be expected to involve progressive unfolding, earlier communications establishing foundations, later ones building on them, the system as a whole exhibiting a developmental arc rather than merely repeating itself.

This progressive character would itself be evidence of intelligent design rather than mechanical transmission. A system that merely repeated the same content indefinitely would not be well matched to recipients whose understanding develops over time.

Unified Without Being Rigid

Continuity requires coherence across time but not uniformity. The communication system could exhibit genuine diversity, addressing different recipients in different circumstances, using different forms and emphases, while remaining unified by consistent underlying commitments.

Internal diversity within an overarching coherence is actually more compelling evidence of a sophisticated source than mechanical uniformity would be.

Transmitted Through Contingent Means

Here an important complication enters. The necessary being communicates to contingent beings, and any communication that persists across time must be transmitted through contingent means: memory, oral tradition, written texts, institutional structures, interpretive communities. All of these are fallible, subject to distortion, and culturally variable.

This creates an inherent tension. The communication originates in a necessary, immutable source but must travel through contingent, mutable carriers. Perfect fidelity of transmission across time cannot be guaranteed by the nature of the carriers alone. This suggests that a rationally designed communication system would include not just content but some mechanism for preserving the integrity of transmission, some way of distinguishing faithful reception from distortion, authentic development from corruption.

What such a mechanism would look like is a further question, but its necessity follows from the tension between immutable source and contingent transmission. A communication system with no such mechanism would be vulnerable to progressive distortion that eventually severed the connection between the original communication and what contingent beings at any given moment actually received.

Distinguishing Development From Contradiction

A continuing communication system would need to navigate the difference between two kinds of change over time:

Legitimate development, later communications building on, deepening, or explicating earlier ones in ways that are continuous with and faithful to what came before. This is expected and valuable, it is how inexhaustible depth becomes progressively accessible.

Contradiction, later communications reversing or denying earlier ones without explanation or resolution. This would be evidence against a unified, immutable source and would undermine the authentication that continuity is supposed to provide.

The distinction between development and contradiction is not always obvious from within the system, it requires interpretive judgment and criteria. But the rational expectation is clear: genuine continuity would exhibit the former and exclude the latter. A communication system that frequently contradicted itself across time would fail to reflect the immutability of its purported source.

Complications That Continuity Creates

The Accumulation of Interpretation

As a communication system persists across time, it inevitably accumulates layers of interpretation, communities of recipients developing traditions of understanding, resolving apparent tensions, applying original communications to new circumstances. This interpretive accumulation is both necessary and dangerous.

It is necessary because the communication system, however orderly, requires active engagement by recipients to be understood and applied. Interpretation is not a distortion of communication but its completion, the communication becomes fully itself only when received and understood.

It is dangerous because interpretive traditions can drift from the original communication, substituting their own concerns and assumptions for what was originally conveyed. The longer the system persists, the more layers of interpretation accumulate, and the more difficult it becomes to distinguish the original communication from its interpretive elaborations.

A rationally designed continuous communication system would therefore need mechanisms not only for preserving its content but for keeping interpretation tethered to what was originally communicated, criteria for distinguishing authentic development from interpretive drift.

The Problem of Apparent Silence

If a continuous communication system is expected, then periods of apparent silence, times when no communication seems to occur, raise questions. Are they evidence against the system's continuity, or can they be accounted for within it?

Several possibilities are consistent with genuine continuity. Silence could itself be communicative, an expected feature of a system that communicates progressively rather than continuously. The communication could be more continuous than it appears, with its presence in certain periods simply less visible to later retrospect. Or the system's continuity might be maintained through the preservation and transmission of earlier communications rather than through constant new ones.

What would be genuinely inconsistent with the rationally expected continuity is not silence per se but irresolvable contradiction, the emergence of communications that cannot be integrated with earlier ones without abandoning the coherence that continuity requires.

The Striking Implication

Following the argument carefully produces a striking result. We began with the bare concept of a necessary being and have derived, step by step, that:

- Such a being could exist and would have specific properties
- It might be intelligent and capable of will
- It would have genuine reasons to communicate with contingent beings
- That communication would be orderly rather than chaotic
- And now: it would persist with continuity across time, developing progressively, transmitted through contingent means but requiring mechanisms to preserve integrity, distinguishing legitimate development from contradiction

This profile is not a description of any arbitrary cultural phenomenon. It is the rational expectation derived from the nature of a necessary being communicating to temporal, rational, contingent recipients. The profile has a remarkably specific shape, and that specificity is itself significant. It narrows considerably the range of what could plausibly be identified as a genuine communication system from a necessary being, were one to exist.

Conclusion

Continuity over time is not merely expected but rationally required of a structured communication system from an intelligent necessary being, for reasons that converge from multiple directions. The immutability of the source demands consistency. The temporality of the recipients demands persistence. The cumulative character of understanding demands progressive development. The need for authentication demands coherence across time. And the universality of the necessary being's purposes demands that the communication be available not just to one generation but to contingent beings as such.

The continuity that would be expected is not simple repetition but progressive, unified development, diverse in form while coherent in substance, transmitted through contingent means while requiring mechanisms to preserve integrity against distortion, distinguishing genuine development from contradiction.

What this establishes is that a genuine communication system from a necessary being would look quite unlike a collection of disconnected religious experiences, cultural traditions, or philosophical insights, however valuable those might be in other respects. It would exhibit the kind of structured, persistent, developing coherence that reflects its origin in a source that does not change. Whether any actual system in human history meets this description is a question that pure reasoning cannot answer. But reasoning has now specified, with some precision, what we would rationally be looking for, and that is no small achievement.

Question 10: Would such a system require an interpretive authority to preserve accuracy?

Question:

Would such a system require an interpretive authority to preserve accuracy?

METHODOLOGY, Mechanism of preservation. Continuity (Q. 9) requires a cause. This question identifies what kind of structure can preserve communication across time without entropy. Texts alone are insufficient (they require interpretation); private judgment is insufficient (it fragments); only a living interpretive authority can maintain identity across centuries. This is the criterion that narrows the field most decisively.

Claude Opus 4.7

This question cuts to one of the most practically consequential points in the entire chain of reasoning, because it asks whether the logic we have been following demands not just a communication system but an institution with authority to interpret it. The answer has implications that are difficult to avoid.

The Problem That Makes the Question Necessary

We identified in the previous exchange a fundamental tension: the communication originates in an immutable, necessary source but must travel through contingent, fallible carriers. This tension does not resolve itself automatically. It generates a specific problem that requires a specific solution.

The problem can be stated precisely. A communication system that:

- Is inexhaustibly deep
- Requires progressive interpretation
- Is transmitted through fallible human means
- Persists across centuries or millennia
- Is addressed to recipients with varying languages, cultures, and circumstances

...will inevitably generate divergent interpretations. This is not a contingent failure of particular recipients but a structural feature of the situation. Divergence is guaranteed by the combination of depth, fallibility, and diversity. The question is not whether divergence will occur but whether it matters and what, if anything, should address it.

Why Divergence Matters

One might argue that interpretive divergence is harmless or even desirable, a sign of the communication's richness rather than a problem to be solved. This position deserves serious consideration before being set aside.

There is genuine truth in it. A communication system of inexhaustible depth will legitimately sustain multiple levels of engagement and multiple valid emphases. Not every difference in interpretation represents error, some represent complementary angles on a reality too large for any single perspective to exhaust.

But this concession has limits. Some interpretive differences are not complementary but contradictory. If interpretation A holds that the necessary being has communicated X, and interpretation B holds that the same system communicates not-X, both cannot be correct. The necessary being's nature, as we have derived it, is not ambiguous on its own terms, it is what it is, necessarily and immutably. A communication from such a source either conveys something determinate or fails to convey anything at all.

If contradictory interpretations are equally authoritative, the communication system effectively communicates nothing, because for every claim it makes, an equally valid counter-claim is available. This collapses the communication into noise, which contradicts the orderliness we established as a rational requirement. A communication system that generates irresolvable contradictions without any mechanism for adjudication has failed at its fundamental purpose.

The Options for Addressing Divergence

1. The Text Alone (Sola Scriptura)

One position holds that the communication system, if it takes textual form, is self-interpreting, sufficiently clear in itself to adjudicate disputed interpretations without any external authority. Recipients engage directly with the text, and correct interpretation emerges from careful, faithful reading.

This position has genuine appeal. It maintains direct access to the original communication, avoids the corruption that any human institution is susceptible to, and treats the communication as truly sufficient for its purposes.

But it faces a structural difficulty that is difficult to overcome. Texts do not interpret themselves. Every reading is conducted by a particular reader in a particular context with particular assumptions. When two careful, faithful readers arrive at contradictory interpretations, the text alone cannot adjudicate between them, because each reader claims the text as the ground of their interpretation. The appeal to the text alone, in cases of genuine dispute, produces not resolution but competing claims each invoking the same authority.

Furthermore, the history of any textual tradition demonstrates empirically that the text-alone approach does not prevent divergence, it multiplies it. Without a mechanism for adjudication, textual traditions fragment progressively, each fragment claiming fidelity to the original. This is not an argument against the value of texts but against the sufficiency of texts alone as a self-regulating system.

2. Individual Reason and Conscience

A related position holds that each recipient, guided by reason and genuine inquiry, can arrive at correct interpretation independently. The communication system addresses individuals as individuals, and each is responsible for their own interpretive engagement.

This preserves epistemic autonomy, a genuine value, and avoids the dangers of institutional authority, which include corruption, self-interest, and the suppression of legitimate development.

But it faces the same structural problem as the text-alone position, compounded. If individual reason is the final arbiter, then contradictory interpretations arrived at by sincere, careful individuals are equally authoritative, which means the communication system produces not determinate content but an indefinitely large set of contradictory claims, none privileged over any other. This is again functional incoherence.

Individual reason is indispensable for engaging with the communication system, but as a final authority for adjudicating disputes, it dissolves the system's communicative function entirely.

3. Community Consensus

Perhaps interpretive authority resides not in any individual or institution but in the consensus of the recipient community over time. What the community consistently holds across diverse circumstances and periods represents the authentic interpretation.

This has genuine advantages. It distributes authority, guards against individual error, and reflects the cumulative wisdom of sustained communal engagement. It also connects interpretation to the living experience of the recipients rather than to abstract textual analysis alone.

But community consensus faces serious difficulties as a sole mechanism. Communities can be wrong, history provides ample evidence that widespread consensus has been confidently mistaken. Consensus can reflect cultural assumptions and power dynamics rather than genuine fidelity to the original communication. And in cases of dispute between communities, appeals to consensus simply relocate the problem, whose consensus is authoritative?

Community consensus is an important input into interpretation but cannot serve as the final adjudicative mechanism without circularity or arbitrariness.

4. A Designated Interpretive Authority

The remaining option is that the communication system itself includes or designates some form of ongoing interpretive authority, an institution or office with the function of preserving the integrity of the communication against distortion and adjudicating genuine disputes.

This is the option most directly implied by the structural analysis, and it is worth following the logic carefully.

Why the Logic Points Toward Designated Authority

The Argument From Purpose

The necessary being communicates for determinate reasons, correcting distortion, enabling relation, promoting flourishing. These purposes are defeated if the communication system generates irresolvable contradictions without adjudication. A rational communicator who anticipates this problem, and an intelligent necessary being surely would, would design the communication system to include a solution to it rather than leaving it unaddressed.

The most direct solution is a designated authority with the function of preserving and authentically interpreting the communication. This is not a supplement to the communication system but part of its rational design.

The Argument From Continuity

We established that continuity over time is rationally required. But continuity of content requires continuity of interpretation, a thread of authentic understanding connecting earlier recipients to later ones. This thread cannot be maintained by texts alone, individual reason alone, or community consensus alone, for the reasons already given.

A designated interpretive authority is what makes continuity of understanding possible across time, not merely continuity of the text but continuity of its faithful reception and application. Without such an authority, continuity of text coexists with fragmentation of meaning, which is continuity in form but not in substance.

The Argument From the Necessary Being's Capacity

If the necessary being is intelligent and has will, and if it has reasons to communicate that extend across time, it has both the capacity and the motivation to ensure its communication is not simply released into contingent transmission and left to drift. An intelligent communicator does not merely initiate communication and then withdraw, particularly when the communication is addressed to beings whose temporal and cognitive limitations make them susceptible to systematic distortion.

Designating an interpretive authority is the kind of provision an intelligent, purposive communicator would make to protect the integrity of what it has communicated. The failure to make such provision would be inconsistent with the communicative intelligence and purpose we have attributed to the necessary being.

The Argument From Authentication

We noted that continuity serves partly as a criterion of authentication, a communication system that maintains coherence across time provides evidence of a unified source. But this authentication function requires that the continuity be real rather than apparent, that what persists is genuine fidelity to the original communication rather than a tradition that has drifted while maintaining the appearance of continuity.

A designated interpretive authority is what distinguishes genuine continuity from apparent continuity. Without it, there is no way to adjudicate between a tradition that has faithfully developed the original communication and one that has gradually substituted its own content while claiming fidelity. Authentication without adjudication is indeterminate.

The Properties Such an Authority Would Need

If the logic demands a designated interpretive authority, we can derive what properties it would need to fulfill its function, again, not from preference but from the requirements of the situation.

Continuity of the Authority Itself

An interpretive authority that existed briefly and then disappeared would not solve the problem of communicative continuity, it would merely relocate it. The authority must itself persist across time, maintaining its function across generations. This implies institutional form, some structure that survives the individuals who instantiate it at any given moment.

Connection to the Original Communication

The authority's interpretations must be tethered to the original communication rather than being free innovation. An authority that simply generates new content without accountability to what was originally communicated would not be preserving the communication but replacing it. Some mechanism connecting the authority's ongoing function to its origin is therefore required, whether through succession, transmission of office, or preserved connection to the founding moment of the communication system.

Scope Defined by Function

The authority's interpretive role would be defined by its function, preserving the integrity of the communication and adjudicating genuine disputes. It would not be unlimited authority over all matters but authority specifically calibrated to this communicative purpose. Overreach beyond this function would itself be a distortion, substituting the authority's own judgments for the content it is meant to preserve.

Distinguishability From the Communication Itself

The authority interprets the communication, it does not replace or supersede it. Recipients must be able to distinguish between the original communication and the authority's interpretations of it, even while relying on the authority to guide their understanding. An authority that made this distinction impossible would be substituting itself for the communication rather than serving it.

Some Form of Guaranteed Integrity

Here the argument reaches its most demanding point. If the interpretive authority is itself composed of contingent, fallible human beings, what prevents it from distorting the communication it is meant to preserve? Institutional self-interest, cultural pressure, and simple error are real and documented features of every human institution.

Two possibilities present themselves. Either the authority operates with a form of assistance from the necessary being that preserves it from certain kinds of error in its definitive interpretive function, a form of ongoing communicative support that is part of the original design of the system. Or the authority's integrity is maintained entirely through human means, careful selection, accountability structures, fidelity to tradition, without any such assistance.

The first option is more consistent with the overall logic. If the necessary being has the intelligence and will to establish a communication system and to designate an interpretive authority, it has the capacity to ensure that authority does not systematically distort the communication it is meant to preserve. An intelligent communicator who designates an authority and then leaves it entirely to its own fallible devices has not solved the problem, it has merely introduced a new contingent link in the chain of transmission.

This does not imply the authority is infallible in all its operations, only that its definitive interpretive function is preserved from the kind of error that would sever the connection between the original communication and what recipients actually receive. The distinction between general fallibility and specific preservational integrity is crucial here.

The Uncomfortable Implication

The logic of this analysis is pushing toward a conclusion that many will find uncomfortable precisely because of its specificity. We began with the bare concept of necessary existence and have derived, step by step:

- A necessary being with specific properties
- The possibility and then the reasons for communication
- The requirement that communication be orderly
- The requirement of continuity over time
- And now: the requirement of a designated interpretive authority with institutional continuity, connection to the original communication, defined scope, and some form of preserved integrity

This is not the profile of a purely private spiritual relationship, or a diffuse religious sentiment, or a philosophical tradition of inquiry. It is the profile of something institutional, historically continuous, and structurally specific.

The argument does not identify which existing institution, if any, meets this description. That is an empirical and historical question that pure reasoning cannot answer. But it has narrowed the field considerably. The rational expectation is not merely that a communication system exists somewhere but that it has a specific, identifiable institutional shape, and that shape is one that most of human religiosity, however sincere, does not exhibit.

Conclusion

A structured communication system from an intelligent necessary being would rationally require some form of designated interpretive authority, for reasons that follow directly from the structural features of the situation rather than from any preference or tradition.

The text alone cannot adjudicate its own disputes. Individual reason alone generates irresolvable fragmentation. Community consensus alone relocates rather than resolves the problem of authority. The purposes of the communication, its required continuity, the intelligence of its source, and the need for genuine authentication all point toward a designated authority with institutional continuity, defined scope, connection to the original communication, and some form of preserved integrity in its definitive function.

The honest conclusion is this: if the chain of reasoning we have followed from necessary existence to communication to continuity is sound, then the communication system we would expect to find in the world is not merely a body of ancient texts or a tradition of spiritual wisdom, it is an ongoing institution with the authority and capacity to say, in concrete cases, what the necessary being has and has not communicated. Whether any such institution exists, and which one it might be, is where philosophy hands the question to history, but philosophy has specified, with considerable precision, what we would be looking for.

Question 11: Given human history, does it seem more likely that multiple contradictory systems are equally true, or that one system preserves the communication more accurately?

Question:

Given human history, does it seem more likely that multiple contradictory systems are equally true, or that one system preserves the communication more accurately?

METHODOLOGY, Application to history. The prior chapters established what rational expectations are. This question turns to the world and asks whether the data of religious history match those expectations. The principle of non-contradiction forbids the claim that contradictory systems are all equally true. So either one preserves communication best, or none does. This forces a comparative evaluation.

Claude Opus 4.7

This is the point where the philosophical argument meets the historical record, and where intellectual honesty requires acknowledging that the question, while still partly philosophical, can no longer be answered by pure reasoning alone. Evidence must be weighed.

What the Prior Reasoning Has Established

Before examining history, it is worth being precise about what the logical chain has already delivered, because it significantly constrains the historical question.

We have derived that a genuine communication system from an intelligent necessary being would exhibit:

- Internal coherence without irresolvable contradiction
- Continuity and institutional persistence across time
- Progressive development that deepens rather than reverses earlier content
- A designated interpretive authority with preserved integrity
- Universal scope, addressed to contingent beings as such, not merely one tribe or era
- Correspondence between its content and the derived properties of the necessary being

This profile functions as a set of criteria against which historical candidates can be assessed. The question is not which system feels most appealing or is most culturally familiar, but which, if any, best satisfies the criteria that rational analysis has generated.

The Prima Facie Case for Multiple Equal Systems

The most common contemporary intuition is that the world's major religious traditions represent equally valid paths to the same ultimate reality, that doctrinal differences are cultural variations on a universal human experience of the transcendent rather than contradictions of which only one can be true.

This view deserves respectful engagement before being assessed critically.

Its strongest points are genuine. All major traditions exhibit:

- Recognition of a reality beyond the contingent order
- Moral frameworks oriented toward something like the good
- Practices of contemplation, self-transcendence, and community
- Profound wisdom about the human condition

These commonalities are real and significant. They suggest that human beings across cultures have been genuinely oriented toward something, that religious experience is not mere illusion but points to a real object.

However, the view that all systems are equally true faces a fundamental logical difficulty that cannot be dissolved by appeal to cultural sensitivity or spiritual generosity. The major traditions do not merely differ in emphasis or cultural expression, they make mutually contradictory claims about the most fundamental questions.

The Contradiction Problem

Consider the central claims in direct confrontation:

On the nature of ultimate reality:

- Classical theism holds that the necessary being is a personal God, one, intelligent, willing, and related to contingent beings
- Advaita Vedanta holds that ultimate reality is impersonal, that the appearance of a personal God is

itself a feature of illusion (*maya*), and genuine knowledge dissolves the distinction between the self and the absolute

- Theravada Buddhism holds that the question of a creator God is either unanswerable or misconceived, what matters is the cessation of suffering, and positing a necessary being may be a category error
- Spinoza's necessary being, embraced by some traditions, is entirely impersonal, with no will, no purpose, and no relation to contingent beings

These are not different cultural expressions of the same claim. They are contradictory. A necessary being cannot simultaneously be personal and impersonal, related and unrelated, one and indistinct from everything. The law of non-contradiction applies here as firmly as anywhere.

On the content of communication:

- Christianity holds that the necessary being became contingent, that the infinite entered the finite in a unique historical event
- Islam holds this claim to be not merely false but the most serious possible theological error, associating partners with God (*shirk*)
- Judaism holds that the messianic claim at the center of Christianity has not been fulfilled
- These three traditions share the most, the same texts, the same concept of a personal creator, and yet make claims that directly exclude each other

On the human condition and its remedy:

- Christianity holds that human beings require redemption from a condition they cannot remedy themselves
- Islam holds that human beings are fundamentally capable of submission and right action without requiring redemption in the Christian sense
- Buddhism holds that the self requiring redemption or submission is itself the illusion to be overcome

Again, these are not complementary perspectives. They diagnose the human condition differently and prescribe irreconcilable responses. At most one diagnosis can be correct.

The conclusion is unavoidable: **multiple contradictory systems cannot all be equally true.** This is not cultural imperialism or religious intolerance, it is elementary logic. Truth excludes its contradictions.

What History Shows About the Candidates

Having established that all systems cannot be equally true, the question becomes which, if any, best satisfies the criteria rational analysis has generated. This requires looking at what history actually shows.

Criterion 1: Institutional Continuity With a Designated Interpretive Authority

Most religious traditions exhibit some form of institutional continuity, but the character of that continuity varies significantly.

Several traditions, particularly those descended from the Abrahamic framework, explicitly claim a chain of interpretive authority traceable to the founding moment of their communication system. Others are more diffuse, collections of texts and practices without a clear mechanism for adjudicating interpretive disputes. Buddhism, for instance, fragmented relatively early into schools with no common authority capable of resolving their differences. Hinduism is extraordinarily diverse, containing within itself positions that contradict each other and no single interpretive institution.

The traditions that most explicitly address the structural requirement of interpretive authority are those claiming an institution with continuous succession from the founding of the communication system.

Criterion 2: Internal Coherence Across Time

Every tradition exhibits internal tensions and historical disputes. The question is whether the tradition has mechanisms for resolving these tensions or merely accumulates them unresolved.

Here a significant distinction emerges. Some traditions have developed elaborate, internally consistent theological and philosophical frameworks, demonstrating that the communication system can sustain rigorous rational engagement without collapsing into contradiction. The medieval synthesis of faith and reason in classical theism, developed across Jewish, Islamic, and Christian traditions, represents perhaps the most sustained example of this kind of coherent development.

Other traditions, while containing profound wisdom, have not produced comparable systematic coherence, or have done so at the cost of fragmenting into schools with no common authority.

Criterion 3: Correspondence With the Derived Properties of the Necessary Being

This criterion is philosophically significant. The reasoning we have conducted across this conversation, deriving properties of the necessary being from necessary existence alone, was conducted without reference to any particular religious tradition. The question is which traditions' descriptions of ultimate reality most closely correspond to what the reasoning independently delivers.

The classical theistic traditions, particularly in their most philosophically developed forms, exhibit striking correspondence. The God of Aquinas, Maimonides, and Avicenna, one, simple, immutable, eternal, the ground of contingent existence, matches the derived profile with remarkable precision. This correspondence is not trivial. It suggests these traditions are tracking the same reality that independent reasoning reaches, rather than projecting culturally conditioned images onto an indifferent universe.

Traditions that describe ultimate reality as impersonal, multiple, or contingent correspond less well to the independently derived profile.

Criterion 4: Universal Scope

The necessary being, as derived, is the ground of all contingent existence, not a tribal deity or a culturally particular phenomenon. A communication from such a being would be expected to address contingent beings universally, not merely one people or civilization.

Some traditions are explicitly particular, addressed to a specific people, with other peoples related only secondarily. Others make explicit universal claims, that the communication is addressed to all human beings without qualification, that its interpretive authority extends to all peoples and times.

Universal scope is a feature of the profile we derived, and traditions that claim it are, to that extent, better candidates than those that do not, though the claim must be assessed against the actual content and history of the tradition, not merely its self-description.

Criterion 5: The Founding Moment and Its Historical Character

A communication system from an intelligent necessary being would be expected to enter history in a way that is distinguishable from purely human religious development. This does not mean it would be obviously miraculous to all observers, but it would be expected to exhibit a character that cannot be fully accounted for by purely naturalistic historical explanation.

Here the assessment becomes most difficult and most contested. Every tradition has a founding narrative that its adherents regard as extraordinary and its critics regard as explicable in human terms. Pure philosophy cannot adjudicate these historical claims, but it can note that the question of the founding moment's character is a genuine and important one, not to be dismissed in either direction.

The More Honest Historical Assessment

Taking all the criteria together, what does the historical record suggest?

It strongly suggests that not all systems are equally true. The contradictions are too fundamental, too central to each tradition's self-understanding, and too resistant

to harmonization to be dissolved by appeals to cultural variation. This conclusion is uncomfortable but unavoidable.

It suggests that the field of serious candidates is narrower than popular pluralism implies. Traditions that lack institutional continuity, designated interpretive authority, universal scope, or correspondence with the independently derived profile of the necessary being are, to that extent, less plausible candidates, regardless of the wisdom and genuine spiritual insight they may contain.

It suggests that the Abrahamic traditions, and particularly their most philosophically developed forms, are the most serious candidates, precisely because they most explicitly address the structural requirements the reasoning has identified. They claim a specific founding moment, a chain of interpretive authority, universal scope, and a description of ultimate reality that corresponds closely to the independently derived profile.

Within the Abrahamic traditions, the differences are themselves significant and not easily harmonized. Judaism, Christianity, and Islam share foundational commitments but make claims that directly contradict each other at crucial points. The question of which, if any, most accurately preserves the communication is one that cannot be answered by philosophy alone, but philosophy can identify what the decisive questions are:

- Whether the interpretive authority claimed is continuous with the founding moment in fact, not merely in assertion

Question 11: Given human history, does it seem more likely that multiple contradictory systems are equally true, or that one system preserves the communication more accurately?

- Whether the doctrinal development across time represents genuine deepening or substantive departure from the original communication
- Whether the central historical claims, the ones that most sharply distinguish the traditions from each other, are historically credible

---

The Limit of the Philosophical Argument

It would be intellectually dishonest to pretend that the chain of reasoning we have followed delivers a clear verdict on which specific tradition, if any, accurately preserves the necessary being's communication. It does not, and claiming otherwise would be a philosophical overreach that undermines the integrity of the entire inquiry.

What the reasoning delivers is:

Negatively, the elimination of the view that all contradictory systems are equally true, and the significant narrowing of the field of plausible candidates based on structural criteria.

Positively, a precise specification of what a genuine communication system would look like, which functions as a framework for historical and theological evaluation rather than a substitute for it.

The reasoning has brought us to the threshold. What lies beyond it, the evaluation of specific historical claims, the assessment of particular founding moments, the judgment of which interpretive tradition has most faithfully preserved what it received, requires exactly the combination of rigorous inquiry and genuine openness that the entire argument has been building toward.

Conclusion

It is not more rational to believe that multiple contradictory systems are equally true. The contradictions are real, fundamental, and logically irresolvable by any appeal to cultural variation or spiritual generosity. Truth excludes its contradictions, and the major traditions contradict each other on questions of the utmost importance.

It is more rational to conclude that at most one system, or perhaps none, accurately preserves the communication, and that the question of which one deserves serious historical and philosophical investigation rather than either uncritical acceptance or dismissive pluralism.

The criteria the reasoning has generated, institutional continuity, designated interpretive authority, internal coherence, correspondence with the independently derived properties of the necessary being, and universal scope, point toward a narrower field of candidates than popular religious pluralism suggests, and toward a more demanding standard of evaluation than either faith alone or skepticism alone typically applies.

Where the argument ultimately points, which specific tradition, if any, meets the full set of criteria, is a question that sits at the boundary of philosophy and history, of reason and evidence, of inquiry and commitment. The most honest thing that can be said is that the question is serious, the criteria are now clear, and the investigation it demands is one of the most important any contingent rational being could undertake.

Question 12: What criteria would be rational for evaluating which system ("most one system" as you say) best preserves an orderly communication from a non-contingent being?

Question:

What criteria would be rational for evaluating which system ("most one system" as you say) best preserves an orderly communication from a non-contingent being?

METHODOLOGY, Evaluative criteria. Before naming candidates, the criteria must be made explicit to avoid circularity. They are drawn directly from the properties established in earlier chapters: metaphysical coherence (Q. 2), continuity (Q. 9), unity of doctrine (Q. 8), and authoritative structure (Q. 10). This rubric will be used to measure traditions in Q. 13–15.

Claude Opus 4.7

This is the right question to ask at this stage, because without explicit criteria, the evaluation of competing systems collapses into preference or cultural familiarity. The criteria must be derived from what the reasoning has already established, not imported from outside.

The criteria fall into several natural groups, moving from the most foundational to the most specific.

Group 1: Criteria Derived From the Nature of the Necessary Being

These are the most fundamental criteria, because they test whether a system's description of ultimate reality corresponds to what independent reasoning has delivered. A system that fails here fails at the root.

1. Correspondence With the Derived Properties

The necessary being, as we derived, is one, simple, immutable, eternal, self-subsistent, uncaused, and the ground of all contingent existence. A system claiming to preserve communication from such a being should describe ultimate reality in ways that correspond to these properties, not perfectly, since the necessary being exceeds full human comprehension, but without straightforward contradiction.

A system that describes ultimate reality as composite, contingent, multiple, or limited fails this criterion at the most basic level. A system that describes it as personal, unified, eternal, and the ground of existence corresponds well, and this correspondence, achieved without borrowing from the philosophical derivation, is itself significant evidence.

2. Coherent Treatment of the Necessary Being's Transcendence and Knowability

We established that the necessary being is categorically beyond full comprehension by contingent minds, yet partially knowable through inference and potentially through communication. A system that accurately preserves the communication should reflect this dual character, neither claiming exhaustive knowledge of the necessary being nor collapsing into complete agnosticism about it.

Systems that describe the necessary being in entirely human terms, as though it were simply a very powerful contingent being, fail to capture the categorical difference derivation establishes. Systems that describe it as entirely unknowable, pure apophasis with no positive content, fail to account for the possibility of genuine communication. The rational system navigates between these failures, maintaining genuine transcendence while affirming genuine, if partial, knowability.

3. Monotheism of the Right Kind

Uniqueness follows from simplicity and infinity, there can be only one necessary being. A system positing multiple ultimate realities, or an ultimate reality that is genuinely composite, fails a criterion derivable from necessary existence alone. This does not exclude complexity of description, it excludes genuine metaphysical pluralism at the ultimate level.

Group 2: Criteria Derived From the Requirements of Communication

These criteria test whether the system exhibits the features that orderly communication from an intelligent necessary being would be expected to have.

4. Internal Coherence and Non-Contradiction

A communication from a being that is truth itself could not be fundamentally self-contradictory. The system's central claims should cohere, not merely avoid surface contradiction but exhibit genuine logical consistency under sustained examination. This does not require that every apparent tension be immediately resolvable, depth generates apparent tensions, but genuine irresolvable contradictions at the core would be disqualifying.

The test here is demanding: not whether adherents claim coherence, but whether the system sustains coherent rational engagement across centuries of rigorous examination without collapsing into contradiction.

5. Stability of Core Content Over Time

We established that the necessary being's immutability implies consistency in its communication. The system's core claims should be identifiably stable across time, recognizable as the same communication received by the earliest recipients and those receiving it now. Development is expected and legitimate; reversal of core commitments is not.

The distinction between development and reversal is crucial and must be applied carefully. Development deepens, explicates, and applies without contradicting. Reversal abandons what was previously held as essential. A system that has undergone genuine reversals on central claims, not peripheral matters but its fundamental account of the necessary being, the human condition, and what is required, fails this criterion.

6. Progressive Coherence of Development

Not only should core content be stable, but the development of the system over time should exhibit internal logic, later developments should be traceable to and continuous with earlier ones. A system whose later doctrines bear no organic relationship to its earlier ones, as though the communication changed its mind wholesale, does not exhibit the continuity we derived as rationally required.

The positive expectation is that later development, while adding to earlier content, should be recognizable as emerging from it, the way a mature understanding of a text, while richer than an initial reading, remains accountable to what the text actually says.

Group 3: Criteria Derived From the Requirements of Institutional Preservation

These criteria test whether the system has the institutional structure required to preserve communicative integrity across time.

7. A Traceable Chain of Interpretive Authority

We established that a designated interpretive authority is rationally required. The system should exhibit a continuous chain of authority traceable from its founding moment to the present, not merely a claim of continuity but a historically identifiable succession. Gaps, ruptures, or reconstructions of the interpretive authority after long discontinuity are significant problems, because they break the chain through which the original communication is preserved.

This criterion is historically investigable. Either the chain of succession is documentable or it is not. Either the authority's connection to the founding moment is traceable or it is asserted without historical grounding.

8. The Authority's Scope Is Defined by the Communication

The interpretive authority exists to serve the communication, to preserve and authentically interpret it, not to replace or supplement it with independent content. A rational criterion is that the authority's scope be defined by and accountable to the communication it interprets, rather than claiming autonomy from it.

A system in which the interpretive authority has effectively replaced the original communication, in which the authority's pronouncements are unaccountable to the content they purport to interpret, has inverted the proper relationship. The authority should be distinguishable from the communication while remaining tethered to it.

9. Mechanisms for Distinguishing Development From Corruption

A system that cannot distinguish between legitimate doctrinal development and corrupting departure from the original communication has no reliable means of self-correction. The rational expectation is that the system contains explicit or implicit criteria for making this distinction, criteria that are themselves accountable to the original communication rather than being freely invented by the interpretive authority.

Systems that treat all change as equally valid, or that have no principled way of ruling out innovations inconsistent with the original communication, fail to provide the preservational function that continuity requires.

Group 4: Criteria Derived From the Expected Character of the Communication Itself

These criteria test the content and character of what the system claims to have received.

10. Correspondence Between Claimed Content and the Necessary Being's Nature

Question 12: What criteria would be rational for evaluating which system ("most one system" as you say) best preserves an orderly communication from a non-contingent being?

The specific content of the purported communication should be consistent with what a necessary being, as derived, could coherently communicate. Claims that the necessary being contradicts its own derived nature, that it is contingent, composite, morally arbitrary, or limited, are internally incoherent. The content of the communication should illuminate and deepen, not contradict, what reasoning independently establishes about the necessary being.

This criterion cuts in a subtle direction. It does not mean the communication must say only what reason already knows, that would make communication superfluous. It means the communication should be consistent with what reason establishes while extending beyond it into territory reason cannot reach alone.

11. The Communication Addresses What Reason Cannot Reach

A genuine communication from a necessary being would be expected to supply precisely what self-discovery cannot, specific intentions, particular relations to contingent beings, the nature of the necessary being's inner life, and guidance about the human condition that goes beyond what philosophical derivation delivers. A system whose content consists entirely of what reason could discover independently provides no evidence of genuine communication from beyond the contingent order.

Conversely, a system whose content is entirely discontinuous with what reason establishes, making no contact with the independently derived properties of the necessary being, provides no basis for evaluating its claims and raises the question of whether it is tracking the necessary being at all or something else entirely.

12. The Moral and Anthropological Framework Coheres With the Nature of Contingent Beings

If the necessary being created contingent beings and communicates with them, its communication about the human condition should correspond to what those beings actually are, their capacities, their limitations, their fundamental orientation. A system whose account of the human condition is demonstrably false, that systematically misrepresents human nature, denies obvious human capacities, or requires beliefs about human beings that are straightforwardly contradicted by experience, lacks the correspondence with reality that a communication from the ground of reality would be expected to exhibit.

Group 5: Historical and Evidential Criteria

These criteria test the historical claims that distinguish systems from one another, particularly the founding moments that each tradition identifies as the origin of its communication.

13. Historical Credibility of the Founding Moment

Every system claiming to preserve a communication from the necessary being grounds that claim in a specific historical founding, a moment or period in which the communication was received and transmitted. The historical credibility of that founding moment is a legitimate criterion of evaluation.

This does not mean the founding moment must be empirically verifiable in every detail by modern historical methods, the nature of what is being claimed often exceeds what such methods are designed to evaluate. But it does mean the founding narrative should not be demonstrably false, should be consistent with what is independently known about the historical context, and should exhibit the kind of historical texture that distinguishes real events from later fabrication.

14. The Character of the Founding Witnesses

The founding moment of any communication system was received and transmitted by specific people. Their character, motivation, and circumstances are historically relevant. Witnesses who had obvious personal incentives to fabricate the founding narrative, power, wealth, social status, provide weaker grounds for confidence than witnesses whose transmission of the communication cost them personally rather than benefiting them.

This criterion does not settle the question alone, sincere witnesses can be sincerely mistaken, but it is a relevant factor in evaluating the probability that what was transmitted reflects what was actually received rather than what the transmitters wished had been received.

15. The Explanatory Adequacy of the Founding Moment

Some founding moments generate effects, institutional, cultural, intellectual, moral, that are difficult to account for without reference to something extraordinary at their origin. A handful of people with no particular social advantages founding a movement that transforms the intellectual and moral landscape of civilizations is not self-explanatory. The explanatory gap between cause and effect is itself a criterion, not conclusive, but relevant.

Systems whose founding moments are entirely explicable by ordinary human social dynamics, where the content of the communication is fully accountable to the cultural context of its origin, provide less evidence of a communication from beyond the contingent order than systems where something about the founding resists ordinary explanation.

Group 6: Meta-Criteria

These final criteria apply to the evaluation process itself rather than to the systems being evaluated.

16. The System's Own Openness to Rational Examination

A genuine communication from an intelligent necessary being would not require its recipients to abandon reason as a condition of reception. We established that self-discovery is the necessary precondition for receiving communication, which means reason is not the enemy of the communication but its indispensable preparation. A system that demands the suspension of rational evaluation as a condition of acceptance is, to that extent, suspect, it is closing off the very faculty by which its claims could be evaluated and authenticated.

This is a delicate criterion. It does not mean the system's content must be fully derivable by reason, it must go beyond reason to be genuine communication. It means the system's core claims should be capable of rational engagement, able to withstand examination without requiring its suppression.

17. Consistency of Application

The criteria must be applied consistently across all candidate systems, including systems one might be predisposed to favor or to reject. A criterion that is applied rigorously to disfavored systems and relaxed for favored ones is not a criterion at all but a rationalization. Intellectual honesty demands that the same standards of historical credibility, internal coherence, institutional continuity, and correspondence with derived properties be applied with equal rigor to every candidate.

This meta-criterion is perhaps the most practically demanding. Every evaluator brings cultural background, personal history, and existing commitments that create systematic biases. Applying the criteria consistently requires ongoing critical self-awareness about where those biases might be distorting the evaluation.

How the Criteria Interact

The criteria do not operate independently, they form a mutually reinforcing structure.

Correspondence with the derived properties of the necessary being establishes the most basic filter. A system that fails here fails regardless of its historical credentials or institutional continuity. Internal coherence and stability over time test whether the system behaves as a genuine communication from an immutable source would be expected to behave. Institutional continuity and interpretive authority test whether the structural requirements of preservation have been met. The character of the founding moment and its witnesses test the historical grounding of the system's claims. And the meta-criteria ensure the evaluation is honest rather than merely sophisticated rationalization.

No single criterion is decisive alone. A system might exhibit strong historical credentials at its founding while exhibiting subsequent doctrinal fragmentation that fails the continuity criterion. A system might maintain remarkable internal coherence while lacking the institutional structure required for preservational integrity. The evaluation requires applying the full set and assessing the overall pattern of correspondence, which is a demanding task, but an honest one.

Conclusion

The rational criteria for evaluating which system best preserves an orderly communication from a necessary being are derivable from what the reasoning has already established, they are not imported from outside but emerge from the internal logic of the inquiry. They fall into six groups: correspondence with the necessary being's derived nature, the features of orderly communication, the requirements of institutional preservation, the expected character of the communication's content, the historical credibility of the founding moment, and the meta-criteria governing honest evaluation.

Applying these criteria is demanding, time-consuming, and resistant to quick resolution, as it should be, given what is at stake. But the criteria themselves are now clear. The next step, actually applying them to specific historical candidates, is one that philosophy can frame but that the inquirer must undertake personally, bringing to it the same rigor and honesty that the argument has demanded at every previous stage.

Question 12: What criteria would be rational for evaluating which system ("most one system" as you say) best preserves an orderly communication from a non-contingent being?

What the reasoning has established, taken as a whole, is that this investigation is not merely intellectually interesting but, given the stakes implied by the existence of a necessary being that grounds all contingent reality, arguably the most important inquiry a contingent rational being can undertake. The criteria are the tools. The investigation remains to be done.

Question 13: Using those criteria, which broad families of religious traditions align most closely with the expected structure?

Question:

Using those criteria, which broad families of religious traditions align most closely with the expected structure?

METHODOLOGY, First-pass filter. Apply the Ch. 12 criteria at the highest level: which broad families of religious traditions remain plausible candidates? This is deliberately coarse; the goal is to eliminate families that cannot, in principle, meet the criteria, not to choose among finalists. Narrows the field to Christianity by structural argument, not preference.

Claude Opus 4.7

This is where the inquiry becomes most consequential, and where intellectual honesty requires applying the criteria rigorously and without favoritism, even when the results are uncomfortable or point in directions that may surprise.

The criteria will be applied systematically to the major families of religious tradition. The goal is not to render a final verdict but to assess the degree of correspondence honestly.

Preliminary Clarification

The criteria fall into a natural priority order for this evaluation:

Question 13: Using those criteria, which broad families of religious traditions align most closely with the expected structure?

Primary criteria, correspondence with the derived properties of the necessary being, and internal coherence. A tradition failing here fails fundamentally, regardless of other merits.

Secondary criteria, institutional continuity, interpretive authority, stability of core content, and progressive development.

Tertiary criteria, historical credibility of the founding moment, character of witnesses, explanatory adequacy.

A tradition must perform reasonably well across all three levels to be a serious candidate. Strong performance on secondary criteria cannot compensate for failure at the primary level.

The Major Families Assessed

1. Dharmic Traditions (Hinduism, Buddhism, Jainism, Sikhism)

Primary Criteria

The Dharmic family is internally diverse to a degree that makes generalization difficult, it encompasses positions from rigorous personal theism (Ramanuja's Vishishtadvaita) to thoroughgoing non-dualism (Shankara's Advaita Vedanta) to explicit rejection of a creator God (classical Buddhism and Jainism). This internal range is itself significant, it means the family does not present a unified answer to the primary question of what ultimate reality is.

Advaita Vedanta comes closest to the derived profile in certain respects, its Brahman is infinite, one, beyond predication, and the ground of all appearance. The via negativa tradition within it is philosophically sophisticated. However, it diverges significantly at a

crucial point: Brahman is ultimately impersonal, and the personal God of devotional Hinduism (Ishvara) is subordinated to an impersonal absolute. On the Advaita account, the appearance of a personal God creating contingent beings is itself part of cosmic illusion. This sits in tension with the derivation, we established that the necessary being's creation of contingent beings is real, not illusory, and that it has genuine reasons for communication.

Theistic Vedanta (Ramanuja, Madhva) corresponds more closely, maintaining a personal God who is genuinely related to contingent beings. But it faces questions about whether its descriptions of ultimate reality avoid the compositeness that necessary existence excludes.

Buddhism in its classical forms explicitly suspends or rejects the question of a creator God. The Buddha's silence on metaphysical questions, including the existence of a necessary being, is not correspondence with the derived profile but deliberate agnosticism about it. Some later Buddhist traditions (particularly certain Mahayana schools) develop something approaching a necessary ground of being, but this represents significant departure from the original teaching rather than its preservation.

Jainism posits multiple eternal souls and rejects a creator God altogether, this fails the primary criterion of correspondence with a unique necessary being that grounds contingent existence.

Sikhism corresponds better at the primary level, its conception of Waheguru as one, transcendent, personal, and the ground of all existence aligns reasonably well with the derived profile. But it emerged late (15th century CE), which raises questions about its relationship to earlier supposed communications.

Secondary Criteria

The Dharmic traditions generally lack the kind of designated interpretive authority the reasoning identifies as structurally required. Hinduism in particular has no single interpretive institution, it is extraordinarily diverse, with competing schools, texts, and traditions lacking any common adjudicative mechanism. Buddhism fragmented early into schools with no common authority. This is a significant weakness at the secondary level.

Tertiary Criteria

The founding moments of the Dharmic traditions are generally less historically documented than the Abrahamic traditions. The Vedic corpus has no clearly identifiable founding moment or witnesses. The Buddha's life is better documented but the transmission of his teaching was immediately contested, producing the early Buddhist councils and subsequent fragmentation.

Assessment

The Dharmic family contains genuine philosophical depth and real correspondence at specific points, particularly in its most sophisticated theistic forms. But the internal diversity at the primary level, the absence of institutional interpretive authority, and the impersonal character of ultimate reality in its most philosophically developed forms represent significant divergences from the derived criteria. The Dharmic traditions are serious philosophical interlocutors but do not, as a family, satisfy the full set of criteria.

---

2. East Asian Traditions (Confucianism, Taoism, Shinto)

Primary Criteria

These traditions are generally less focused on the metaphysical question of a necessary being and more concerned with the ordering of human life, society, and relationship to nature.

Taoism comes closest to engaging the primary question, the Tao as the unnameable, eternal ground of all things has genuine resonances with the derived profile. The opening of the Tao Te Ching, that the Tao which can be named is not the eternal Tao, reflects genuine apophatic insight. But the Tao is impersonal, without intelligence or will in any meaningful sense, and does not communicate. It is more analogous to Spinoza's necessary nature than to the intelligent, communicating necessary being the reasoning points toward.

Confucianism is primarily ethical and social rather than metaphysical, it does not centrally address the existence or nature of a necessary being. **Shinto** is polytheistic and nature-oriented, it fails the primary criterion of uniqueness derivable from necessary existence.

Secondary and Tertiary Criteria

None of these traditions claims the kind of designated interpretive authority the reasoning requires, or a specific founding moment of communication from a necessary being in the relevant sense.

Assessment

The East Asian family, with the partial exception of philosophical Taoism, does not seriously engage the question of a necessary being in the terms the derivation generates. These traditions contain genuine wisdom but do not present themselves as, and do not structurally resemble, preserved communications from an intelligent necessary being directed at contingent beings universally. They largely fail at the primary level.

---

3. Indigenous and Animist Traditions

Primary Criteria

These traditions are enormously diverse and resist generalization. Many involve a supreme being or creator above lesser spirits, which has genuine correspondence at the primary level. The widespread human intuition of a supreme reality, found across unconnected cultures, is philosophically significant and should not be dismissed.

However, most indigenous traditions do not claim universal scope, they are addressed to particular peoples in particular places, not to contingent beings as such. Many involve genuine metaphysical pluralism, multiple spirits, forces, or beings, that fails the uniqueness criterion.

Secondary and Tertiary Criteria

Indigenous traditions generally lack institutional interpretive authority of the kind required, and their founding moments are typically prehistoric and undocumentable. Oral transmission across generations is extraordinarily susceptible to the cumulative distortion that a designated interpretive authority is designed to prevent.

Assessment

Indigenous traditions may preserve genuine, if fragmentary, awareness of the necessary being, which would be expected if the necessary being is the ground of all contingent existence and human beings are naturally oriented toward it. But they do not, as a family, satisfy the structural criteria for being a preserved communication system. They are more plausibly understood as natural human orientation toward the necessary being, which is expected, than as preserved communication from it.

---

4. The Abrahamic Family (Judaism, Christianity, Islam)

This family requires the most extended treatment because it most directly addresses the criteria the reasoning has generated.

What the Family Shares

The Abrahamic traditions share a foundational structure that corresponds remarkably well to the derived profile at the primary level:

- A single, unique necessary being, personal, intelligent, willing, eternal, the creator of contingent existence
- Universal scope, the necessary being is not a tribal deity but the ground of all reality
- A specific historical communication, not merely philosophical inference but claimed direct disclosure
- An explicit interpretive tradition with designated authority
- A moral and anthropological framework treating contingent beings as genuinely significant to the necessary being

This shared structure is the reason the Abrahamic family, taken together, is the most serious candidate for satisfying the full set of criteria. The correspondence at the primary level is not superficial, it reflects the same convergence with the independently derived profile that we noted for classical theism generally.

The question is which branch of the family, if any, best satisfies the complete set of criteria, because the branches make mutually contradictory claims that cannot all be true simultaneously.

Judaism

Primary Criteria

Judaism's conception of God corresponds closely to the derived profile, one, personal, eternal, the creator of contingent existence, the source of moral order. Classical Jewish philosophy, particularly Maimonides, developed a sophisticated account of divine unity, simplicity, and transcendence that aligns precisely with what necessary existence entails. The via negativa in Jewish thought is among the most rigorous in any tradition.

Secondary Criteria

Judaism has maintained remarkable continuity of core content across more than three millennia, a historical achievement without parallel. The rabbinic tradition represents a genuine interpretive authority with defined scope, developed after the destruction of the Temple as a sophisticated mechanism for preserving and applying the communication without the earlier institutional structures. The development from biblical to rabbinic Judaism exhibits the character of legitimate development, deepening and applying without reversing core commitments.

However, Judaism's interpretive authority is distributed across the rabbinic tradition rather than concentrated in a single ongoing institution with universal jurisdiction. There is no single body capable of issuing definitive rulings binding on all Jews, the closest approximations (Sanhedrin) ceased to function in late antiquity and have not been reconstituted. This is a real weakness at the secondary criterion level, though Judaism compensates through the extraordinary stability of its textual tradition and the remarkable coherence of rabbinic interpretation across centuries and geographies.

Tertiary Criteria

The historical credibility of Judaism's founding, the Mosaic covenant and the events at Sinai, is better documented than most ancient religious founding moments but has been subjected to significant historical scrutiny. The tradition's self-understanding involves a communication received by an entire people rather than a single individual, which addresses some concerns about individual witness credibility. The survival of the Jewish people across extraordinary historical adversity, exile, persecution, diaspora, while maintaining doctrinal coherence is a phenomenon that resists simple naturalistic explanation.

Notable Weakness

Judaism's explicit particularity, the communication is addressed primarily to a chosen people, with universal scope implied but not fully developed institutionally, sits in some tension with the universality criterion. The tradition contains genuinely universal elements but has not historically claimed a universal institutional mission.

Islam

Primary Criteria

Islam's conception of God (Allah) corresponds closely to the derived profile, absolutely one, without partners, eternal, the creator of all contingent existence. Islamic theology, particularly in the Ash'ari and Maturidi schools, developed sophisticated accounts of divine unity and transcendence. The rejection of any association of partners with God (shirk) reflects genuine philosophical commitment to the uniqueness entailed by necessary existence.

Secondary Criteria

Islam claims a specific, identifiable founding moment, the revelation to Muhammad, and a designated interpretive community. The rapid development of Islamic jurisprudence (fiqh) and theology (kalam) represents a serious attempt to apply the communication systematically. Universal scope is explicit and central, the Quran presents itself as addressed to all humanity, and Islam's missionary character reflects this universality.

However, Islam fragmented relatively early into competing interpretive traditions (Sunni and Shia, and further subdivisions within each) with no single authority capable of adjudicating disputes binding on all Muslims. This fragmentation, occurring within the first generation of the founding, is a significant weakness at the secondary criterion level. Unlike Christianity, which developed conciliar and later papal mechanisms for adjudicating disputes before major fragmentation, Islam's early fragmentation left the interpretive authority question structurally unresolved.

Tertiary Criteria

The historical credibility of the founding moment is strong in some respects, Muhammad is a well-documented historical figure, the transmission of the Quran was carefully guarded from an early date, and the early Islamic community's rapid expansion is historically remarkable. The character of the founding witnesses, early Muslims who accepted significant personal cost for their convictions, satisfies the criterion of witnesses without obvious personal incentive for fabrication.

Notable Weakness

Islam's relationship to the prior Abrahamic communications is complex. It explicitly claims to correct distortions in Judaism and Christianity, which requires the prior traditions to have been corrupted. Whether this corruption occurred is historically investigable, and the evidence is contested. If the prior traditions were not corrupted in the ways Islam claims, Islam's claim to be the corrective final communication faces significant challenges.

Christianity

Primary Criteria

Christianity's conception of God corresponds closely to the derived profile at the level of the classical tradition, one, eternal, simple, the ground of contingent existence. Classical Christian theology, particularly in its Nicene and Chalcedonian formulations, developed a sophisticated account of divine nature that corresponds well to what necessary existence entails.

Christianity introduces a claim that goes beyond anything derivable from necessary existence alone, that the necessary being became contingent, entering history in a particular human life. This claim cannot be derived from the prior reasoning, it is precisely the kind of particular, specific content that genuine communication from a necessary being would be expected to add beyond what reason can reach. It is either the most extraordinary truth or the most consequential error in human intellectual history. It cannot be dismissed as peripheral.

Secondary Criteria

Christianity most explicitly addresses the structural requirement of a designated interpretive authority. The claim to apostolic succession, a traceable chain of interpretive authority from the founding moment, is historically identifiable in a way that is verifiable or falsifiable by historical investigation. The development of conciliar mechanisms for adjudicating disputes, and subsequently the development of more concentrated interpretive authority in certain branches, represents the most direct institutional response to the structural requirement the reasoning identifies.

The development of Christian doctrine exhibits, in its classical form, the character of legitimate progressive development, the Trinitarian and Christological definitions of the early councils represent explicitation and defense of what was already implicit in the founding communication rather than reversal of it. The continuity between the earliest Christian testimony and subsequent doctrinal development is traceable in a way that is historically documentable.

Tertiary Criteria

The historical credibility of Christianity's founding moment, the life, death, and resurrection of Jesus, is the most extensively investigated founding claim in any religious tradition. The evidence is contested but not negligible. Several features satisfy the tertiary criteria:

The founding witnesses, those who transmitted the resurrection claim, had no obvious personal incentive for fabrication, and many paid significant personal costs for their testimony. The explanatory gap between the historical situation of a small, failed messianic movement after its leader's execution and the subsequent transformation of the Roman world is among the most discussed and debated phenomena in historical scholarship. The earliest testimony to the central claim is closer in time to the founding moment than is typical for ancient religious movements.

Notable Tensions

Christianity's internal fragmentation, Eastern and Oriental Orthodoxy, Roman Catholicism, and the many Protestant traditions, raises the institutional continuity question acutely. If the designated interpretive authority is required, and if Christianity most explicitly claims one, then the fragmentation of that authority is a serious problem. It demands evaluation of which branch, if any, maintains genuine continuity with the founding moment's interpretive structure.

The Second-Order Question: Within Christianity

Since Christianity most explicitly addresses the interpretive authority criterion, its internal divisions deserve specific attention under the criteria.

The Eastern Orthodox tradition claims apostolic succession, conciliar authority, and stability of core content with remarkable fidelity to the patristic tradition. Its weakness is the absence of a single continuing institution with universal jurisdiction, it is a communion of autocephalous churches without a universal adjudicating authority.

The Roman Catholic tradition claims not only apostolic succession but a specific continuing office, the papacy, with universal jurisdiction and defined preservational integrity in its definitive teaching function. This is the most direct institutional response to the structural requirement the reasoning identifies. Whether the historical claim of continuous succession is accurate is investigable; whether the claimed preservational integrity is credible is a theological and philosophical question of the first order.

The Protestant traditions generally reject the designated interpretive authority criterion in favor of the text-alone position. We already established that this position faces a structural difficulty, texts do not interpret themselves, and the appeal to scripture alone has historically produced fragmentation rather than resolution of interpretive disputes. This does not mean Protestant traditions contain no truth, but it does mean they do not satisfy the institutional criterion the reasoning identifies as structurally required.

The Overall Assessment

Applying the criteria systematically produces a result that is more determinate than popular pluralism allows but more cautious than any single tradition's adherents typically claim.

The Dharmic, East Asian, and Indigenous families, while containing genuine insight and real philosophical value, do not satisfy the full set of criteria. They fail primarily at the level of correspondence with the necessary being's derived properties (particularly the

personal, communicating character), institutional continuity, and interpretive authority.

The Abrahamic family satisfies the primary criteria most fully, its conception of ultimate reality corresponds most closely to what necessary existence independently entails, it claims specific historical communication, it addresses the interpretive authority requirement explicitly, and it exhibits universal scope.

Within the Abrahamic family, the traditions diverge significantly. Judaism satisfies the primary criteria fully and exhibits extraordinary continuity, but its distributed interpretive authority and explicit particularity are weaknesses. Islam satisfies the primary criteria and exhibits universal scope, but its early fragmentation of interpretive authority and its dependence on the claim that prior traditions were corrupted are significant challenges. Christianity satisfies the primary criteria, most directly addresses the institutional requirement, and its founding moment is the most extensively investigated, but its internal fragmentation raises the question of which branch genuinely preserves the interpretive continuity it claims.

Within Christianity, the traditions that most explicitly satisfy the interpretive authority criterion, those claiming apostolic succession with institutional continuity, correspond most closely to the structural requirement the reasoning identifies. Among these, the tradition claiming the most concentrated and clearly defined interpretive authority with universal jurisdiction corresponds most precisely to what the reasoning demands.

Question 13: Using those criteria, which broad families of religious traditions align most closely with the expected structure?

What This Assessment Does and Does Not Establish

This assessment establishes a ranking of correspondence with the derived criteria, it does not establish which tradition is true. That final step requires:

- Detailed historical investigation of the specific founding claims
- Careful evaluation of the evidence for and against the central historical assertions of each tradition
- Personal engagement with the tradition that most closely satisfies the criteria

What the assessment does establish is that the investigation is not arbitrary, the criteria generate a determinate direction. The inquiry points toward the Abrahamic family generally, toward the traditions within that family that most explicitly address the institutional requirement, and within those toward the branch that most directly satisfies the interpretive authority criterion in its concentrated and historically continuous form.

A genuinely rational inquirer following this argument to its conclusion would not find all traditions equally worthy of investigation. The criteria narrow the field significantly, not to a single certain answer, but to a serious and identifiable candidate that deserves the most careful and sustained examination a contingent rational being can give it.

That is as far as the philosophical argument can honestly take the inquiry. The rest belongs to the investigator.

Question 14: Among those families ("within Christianity" as you say), which traditions maintain "apostolic succession with institutional continuity" as you say?

Question:

Among those families ("within Christianity" as you say), which traditions maintain "apostolic succession with institutional continuity" as you say?

METHODOLOGY, Second-pass filter. Within the surviving family (Q. 13), apply the criterion of apostolic succession and institutional continuity, both required by Q. 9–10. This eliminates traditions that originated as ruptures or that lack continuous interpretive authority. The set of candidates narrows to those with documented continuity from the apostolic foundation.

Claude Opus 4.7

This question calls for careful historical analysis rather than philosophical derivation, we have moved from what the reasoning demands to what history actually shows. The answer is more determinate than many assume.

What Apostolic Succession With Institutional Continuity Means

Before identifying which traditions claim and maintain it, the concept needs precision, because the term is used with varying degrees of rigor.

Apostolic succession in the full sense requires:

- **Continuity of office**, a traceable chain of ordained ministers from the apostles to the present, with no breaks requiring reconstruction from outside the chain
- **Continuity of community**, the institutional church persisting as a recognizable body, not merely individual lineages of ordination
- **Continuity of teaching**, the core content preserved and transmitted through the succession, not merely the formal chain
- **Universal or at least principled scope**, the succession functioning as a genuine interpretive authority, not merely a local or regional phenomenon

With these requirements in mind, the field narrows considerably.

The Traditions That Claim It

Several distinct families claim apostolic succession with institutional continuity. They fall into three broad groups.

Question 14: Among those families ("within Christianity" as you say), which traditions maintain "apostolic succession with institutional continuity" as you say?

Group 1: The Roman Catholic Church

The Roman Catholic Church presents the most historically extensive and institutionally concentrated claim to apostolic succession.

What it claims:

- Unbroken succession of bishops from the apostles, with the Bishop of Rome (pope) holding primacy as successor of Peter
- A continuous institutional identity from the apostolic community to the present
- A defined mechanism, the papal magisterium and ecumenical councils, for preserving and authentically interpreting the communication
- Universal jurisdiction, the authority extends in principle to all contingent beings, not merely a regional or ethnic community

Historical assessment of the claim: The historical continuity of the Roman episcopate from the earliest centuries is better documented than almost any other ancient institution. Lists of Roman bishops from the late second century onward are historically identifiable. The institutional continuity of the Roman church through the patristic period, the medieval period, the Reformation, and modernity is a matter of historical record rather than mere assertion.

The claim faces genuine historical challenges, the precise nature of Petrine primacy in the earliest period is debated, the development of papal authority was gradual rather than fully explicit from the beginning, and the period of multiple claimants to the papacy (the Western Schism, 1378-1417) raises questions about continuity that Catholic historians have addressed but that remain subjects of scholarly discussion.

Correspondence with the structural criterion: Of all existing institutions, the Roman Catholic Church most directly satisfies the criterion of a designated interpretive authority with concentrated, continuing, universal jurisdiction and defined preservational integrity. The First Vatican Council's definition of papal infallibility (1870) represents the most explicit institutional claim to the kind of preservational integrity the reasoning identified as structurally required, the claim that when the pope speaks definitively on matters of faith and morals, the communication is preserved from the kind of error that would sever the connection between what is taught and what was originally communicated.

Whether this claim is true is a separate question from whether it satisfies the structural criterion, it does satisfy it, more directly than any alternative.

Group 2: The Eastern Orthodox Churches

The Eastern Orthodox family, comprising the Ecumenical Patriarchate of Constantinople, the Russian Orthodox Church, the Greek Orthodox Church, the Antiochian Orthodox Church, the Serbian, Romanian, Bulgarian, Georgian, and other autocephalous churches, claims apostolic succession with a different institutional structure.

Question 14: Among those families ("within Christianity" as you say), which traditions maintain "apostolic succession with institutional continuity" as you say?

What it claims:

- Unbroken succession of bishops from the apostles in each of the ancient apostolic sees, Constantinople, Alexandria, Antioch, Jerusalem, and others
- Preservation of the authentic tradition through the seven Ecumenical Councils (325-787 CE) and the continuing consensus of the episcopate
- The fullness of the faith expressed through conciliar rather than monarchical authority
- Self-understanding as the continuation of the undivided church of the first millennium

Historical assessment of the claim: The historical credibility of Eastern Orthodox apostolic succession is generally regarded as strong, the ancient sees have continuous episcopal lists comparable to Rome's, and the patristic tradition on which Orthodoxy draws is shared with and often better preserved in the East than in the West. The seven Ecumenical Councils are accepted as authoritative by virtually all traditions claiming apostolic succession, making this the area of broadest consensus.

The Eastern churches did not experience the Reformation's disruption of succession and have maintained liturgical and theological continuity with the patristic period in ways that are historically documentable.

Correspondence with the structural criterion: Eastern Orthodoxy satisfies the apostolic succession criterion in its episcopal dimension but addresses the interpretive authority criterion differently from Rome. Authority is conciliar, residing in the consensus of bishops gathered in council, rather than concentrated in a single continuing office. This raises the question of how disputes are adjudicated when no council is convened or when councils are contested. The practical difficulty of convening an authoritative pan-Orthodox council has been demonstrated historically, the most recent attempt (Crete, 2016) was boycotted by several major Orthodox churches, limiting its authority.

The absence of a single continuing office with universal jurisdiction is a real weakness relative to the structural criterion, though Eastern Orthodoxy would argue that conciliar authority better reflects the nature of the church than papal monarchy.

Group 3: The Oriental Orthodox Churches

The Oriental Orthodox family, comprising the Coptic Orthodox Church, the Ethiopian Orthodox Tewahedo Church, the Syriac Orthodox Church, the Armenian Apostolic Church, the Malankara Orthodox Syrian Church, and others, separated from the broader church following the Council of Chalcedon (451 CE) over Christological definitions.

What it claims:

- Apostolic succession traceable to the apostolic period, the Coptic Church to St. Mark, the Armenian Church to Thaddaeus and Bartholomew, the Ethiopian Church to the apostolic mission
- Preservation of the authentic tradition as received before the Chalcedonian controversy
- Continuity of the ancient apostolic sees in their original territories

Historical assessment of the claim: The historical credibility of Oriental Orthodox apostolic succession is generally recognized, these churches have maintained continuous episcopal succession in their regions from the early centuries. The Coptic Church in particular represents one of the oldest continuously existing Christian communities, with a documented history extending to the earliest centuries of Christianity.

Correspondence with the structural criterion: The Oriental Orthodox churches satisfy the apostolic succession criterion in its episcopal dimension but share with Eastern Orthodoxy the absence of a single universal interpretive authority. Additionally, their separation from the broader church at Chalcedon raises the question of whether their preservation of the tradition is complete, whether the Christological definitions they rejected represent legitimate development of the original communication or its distortion.

Group 4: Some Anglican and Old Catholic Churches

These traditions claim apostolic succession but occupy a more contested position.

The Anglican Communion claims apostolic succession through the continuity of episcopal ordination from the pre-Reformation English church. However, this claim is rejected by Rome (Leo XIII's Apostolicae Curae, 1896, declared Anglican orders invalid) and disputed by others, on the grounds that the Reformation-era revisions to ordination rites introduced a break in the

succession. Eastern Orthodoxy has generally not recognized Anglican orders either.

The Anglican claim is also complicated by its internal diversity, the Anglican Communion contains positions ranging from near-Catholic to near-Protestant, without a clear mechanism for adjudicating which represents the authentic tradition.

The Old Catholic Churches (those that separated from Rome following Vatican I's definition of papal infallibility) claim valid apostolic succession, a claim generally recognized as historically credible in terms of the episcopal lineage. However, their small size, regional character, and subsequent theological development raise questions about whether they satisfy the institutional continuity criterion in its full sense.

The Comparison on the Structural Criterion

Returning to the criterion the reasoning identified as most demanding, a designated interpretive authority with institutional continuity, defined scope, and some form of preserved integrity in its definitive function, the traditions can be ranked:

Most directly satisfying the criterion: The Roman Catholic Church, it alone claims a single, continuing, universal interpretive office with explicitly defined preservational integrity. The claim may be false, but it is the claim that most precisely matches what the reasoning identified as structurally required.

Substantially satisfying the criterion: The Eastern Orthodox churches, they satisfy the episcopal succession criterion and the conciliar authority criterion, but the absence of a single universal adjudicating authority leaves the interpretive function incomplete relative to what the reasoning demands.

The Oriental Orthodox churches, similar to Eastern Orthodoxy, with the additional question raised by the Chalcedonian separation.

Partially satisfying the criterion: The Anglican Communion, the succession claim is contested and the internal diversity is unresolved.

The Old Catholic churches, the succession is credible but the institutional presence is minimal.

Not satisfying the criterion: All Protestant traditions that explicitly reject apostolic succession and/or the designated interpretive authority in favor of scripture alone, individual conscience, or community consensus. These traditions may contain genuine insight and authentic Christian elements, but they do not satisfy the structural criterion the reasoning identified as required, and many of them explicitly acknowledge this, framing their rejection of interpretive authority as a principled theological position rather than a deficiency.

The Internal Logic of the Assessment

What emerges from applying the criterion consistently is a nested structure:

Among all religious families, the Abrahamic traditions correspond most closely to the derived criteria.

Among the Abrahamic traditions, Christianity most explicitly addresses the interpretive authority requirement.

Among Christian traditions, those claiming apostolic succession with institutional continuity, Catholic, Eastern Orthodox, and Oriental Orthodox, satisfy the structural criterion more fully than those that do not.

Among those claiming apostolic succession, the Roman Catholic Church most directly satisfies the specific form of the criterion the reasoning identified, a single, continuous, universal interpretive office with defined preservational integrity.

This does not establish that the Roman Catholic Church's claims are true. It establishes that its claims, if true, would most precisely satisfy what the reasoning has identified as structurally required. The question of whether the claims are true, whether the historical founding moment is credible, whether the succession is genuine, whether the development of doctrine represents authentic deepening or distortion, whether the defined preservational integrity is real, is a further investigation that the philosophical argument cannot complete but has now framed with considerable precision.

What the Honest Inquirer Now Faces

The philosophical argument has delivered as much as philosophical argument can deliver. It has:

- Derived the properties of a necessary being
- Established the rationality of communication from such a being
- Specified the structural requirements of a genuine communication system
- Assessed the major religious families against those requirements

Question 14: Among those families ("within Christianity" as you say), which traditions maintain "apostolic succession with institutional continuity" as you say?

- Identified the Abrahamic family as most corresponding
- Within that family, identified Christianity as most directly addressing the institutional requirement
- Within Christianity, identified the traditions claiming apostolic succession as most satisfying the criterion
- Within those traditions, identified the Roman Catholic claim as most precisely matching the structural requirement

The inquiry now stands at a threshold that philosophical reasoning cannot cross. What lies beyond it involves:

- Historical investigation of the specific claims to apostolic succession and their credibility
- Evaluation of the founding moment, the life, death, and resurrection of Jesus, and the evidence for and against it
- Assessment of whether doctrinal development represents authentic deepening or corruption
- Engagement with the actual content of the tradition, not merely its structure but what it claims the necessary being has communicated

These are investigations that require more than philosophical analysis. They require the kind of sustained, honest, personal engagement that the argument has been building toward from the beginning. The philosophical chain that began with the question of whether a non-contingent being can exist has arrived, by steps each of which is defensible on its own terms, at the door of a specific historical institution making specific historical claims.

Whether the inquirer opens that door, and what they find if they do, is no longer a matter of philosophy alone.

Question 15: Based purely on metaphysical coherence, historical continuity, unity of doctrine, and authoritative structure, which specific tradition best fits the expected characteristics of an orderly communication from a non-contingent being?

Question:

Based purely on metaphysical coherence, historical continuity, unity of doctrine, and authoritative structure, which specific tradition best fits the expected characteristics of an orderly communication from a non-contingent being?

METHODOLOGY, Final identification. All four criteria from Q.12 are now applied simultaneously to the remaining candidates from Q.14. The question is structured to prevent ad hoc reasoning: the criteria were fixed before the candidates were named, and the candidates were narrowed by structural argument. The answer is whichever tradition uniquely satisfies all four. This is the terminus of the chain, the question every prior chapter was preparing for.

Claude Opus 4.7

This is the question the entire chain of reasoning has been building toward. The criteria have been established, the families assessed, the traditions within the leading family examined. Intellectual honesty now requires stating the conclusion directly rather than indefinitely deferring it.

The Conclusion the Argument Delivers

On the four criteria specified, metaphysical coherence, historical continuity, unity of doctrine, and authoritative structure, one tradition corresponds most closely to the expected characteristics of an orderly communication from a non-contingent being.

That tradition is Roman Catholicism.

This conclusion is not asserted from faith or cultural preference. It follows from applying the criteria the reasoning has generated to the historical record. Each criterion will be addressed in turn to show why this conclusion follows and where its limits lie.

Criterion 1: Metaphysical Coherence

The question here is whether the tradition's account of ultimate reality corresponds to the properties independently derived from necessary existence, unity, simplicity, immutability, aseity, eternality, and the ground of all contingent being.

Roman Catholic theology, in its classical form developed by Aquinas and the subsequent Thomistic tradition, corresponds with extraordinary precision to the independently derived profile. The God of classical Catholic theism is:

- Absolutely one and simple, not composed of parts, not a being among beings but the ground of being itself
- Immutable and eternal, outside time, not subject to change
- Self-subsistent, existing through its own nature, dependent on nothing
- The uncaused cause of all contingent existence

This is not a coincidence of terminology. The Thomistic synthesis explicitly derives these properties through the same kind of metaphysical reasoning this conversation has followed, from the distinction between contingent and necessary existence, through the requirements of simplicity and immutability, to the conclusion that the necessary being is the unrestricted act of existence itself (*ipsum esse subsistens*).

The correspondence between the Thomistic account and the independently derived profile is as close as any philosophical system has achieved. No other religious tradition has produced a metaphysical account of ultimate reality that corresponds so precisely to what the logic of necessary existence independently demands.

Qualification: Eastern Orthodoxy and classical Judaism reach similar conclusions at the primary level, Maimonides and the Eastern Fathers share the commitment to divine simplicity, unity, and transcendence. The metaphysical coherence criterion does not sharply distinguish Roman Catholicism from these traditions at the level of the concept of God. The differentiation occurs more clearly at the secondary criteria.

Criterion 2: Historical Continuity

The question here is whether a traceable, unbroken chain of institutional presence and succession connects the tradition to its founding moment without reconstructions, fabrications of continuity, or gaps requiring the tradition to reinvent itself.

Roman Catholicism's historical continuity from the apostolic period to the present is among the most extensively documented of any institution in human history. Several features of this continuity are significant:

Episcopal succession: The list of Roman bishops from the late second century onward is historically identifiable. The tradition of Petrine primacy, the special authority of the Roman see, is attested in early Christian documents (Clement of Rome, Ignatius of Antioch, Irenaeus of Lyon) within living memory of the apostolic period. The claim is not without historical complexity, but it is not a later fabrication.

Institutional persistence: The Roman Catholic Church has maintained continuous institutional identity through the fall of the Western Roman Empire, the medieval period, the Reformation, the Enlightenment, the French Revolution, and modernity, each of which posed existential challenges to the institution. No comparable institution has maintained continuous identity across so wide a historical range.

Textual and liturgical continuity: The core texts, liturgical structures, and doctrinal formulations of Roman Catholicism connect identifiably to the patristic period. The Nicene Creed, the canon of scripture, the structure of the sacramental system, all are traceable to the early centuries with documented historical continuity.

Genuine challenges to the continuity claim:

- The development of papal authority was gradual, claims made in the high medieval papacy go beyond what is explicitly present in the earliest documents
- The Western Schism (1378-1417), during which multiple claimants competed for the papacy, raises questions about institutional continuity at a formal level that Catholic historians have addressed but that deserve honest acknowledgment
- The relationship between the pre-Nicene church and later Catholic developments is contested, Protestant historians argue the continuity is less clean than Catholic accounts suggest

These challenges are real but do not, on balance, break the continuity claim. Every ancient institution has periods of internal crisis. The question is whether the institution persisted through those crises as a recognizable continuation of what preceded them, and the historical record supports continuity more than rupture.

Comparison with Eastern Orthodoxy: Eastern Orthodoxy has equally credible apostolic succession in its ancient sees and arguably better preserves certain patristic traditions. Its weakness on this criterion is not the absence of historical continuity but the absence of a single continuing institutional center, it is a communion of autocephalous churches, and its unity is more doctrinal and spiritual than institutional.

Criterion 3: Unity of Doctrine

The question here is whether the tradition has maintained stable, consistent core content across time, developing without reversing, deepening without contradicting, preserving what was originally communicated against cumulative distortion.

This is perhaps the most demanding criterion because it requires distinguishing legitimate development from substantive departure. The framework for making this distinction, developed most rigorously by John Henry Newman in his *Essay on the Development of Christian Doctrine*, identifies several marks of genuine development: preservation of type, continuity of principles, power of assimilation, logical sequence, anticipation of future developments, conservative action upon the past, and chronic vigor.

Where Roman Catholicism performs strongly:

The core doctrinal content of Roman Catholicism, the Trinity, the Incarnation, the Resurrection, the sacramental system, the moral framework, has remained stable across two millennia in a way that is historically remarkable. The Nicene Creed of 325 CE, the Chalcedonian definition of 451 CE, and the subsequent doctrinal tradition develop the original apostolic proclamation in ways that are traceable and internally consistent.

The Catholic tradition has repeatedly demonstrated the capacity to absorb philosophical challenges, Aristotelianism in the medieval period, Enlightenment rationalism, and modern historical criticism, while maintaining doctrinal core stability. This absorption without reversal is the mark of a tradition with genuine preservational integrity rather than one that simply reflects its cultural environment.

Where the criterion reveals tension:

The development of Marian dogmas, the Immaculate Conception (defined in 1854) and the Assumption (defined in 1950), are instances where Catholic development has been contested even by sympathetic observers. Whether these represent legitimate development of what was implicit in the original communication or additions that go beyond it is a serious theological question. Catholic theology offers an account of its development; Eastern Orthodox and Protestant critics argue that the account is insufficient.

The history of the papacy itself includes periods, particularly in the medieval and Renaissance periods, where the institution's behavior was difficult to reconcile with its claimed function. Catholic theology distinguishes between the institution's preservation of doctrinal integrity and the personal failures of its officers, a distinction that is coherent but requires careful application.

Comparison: Eastern Orthodoxy can claim comparable doctrinal stability, particularly in its fidelity to the seven Ecumenical Councils. Its advantage is that it has not made the further doctrinal developments that create questions for Catholicism. Its disadvantage is that this conservatism comes partly from the absence of a mechanism for authoritative doctrinal development, which means genuine questions raised by historical development remain, in practice, unresolved.

Judaism achieves remarkable doctrinal stability across an even longer period, but its stability is partly a function of not having to address the specific claims that Christianity and Islam raise, since it predates and does not accept them.

Criterion 4: Authoritative Structure

This is the criterion on which Roman Catholicism most decisively distinguishes itself from all competitors. The reasoning established that a genuine communication system requires a designated interpretive authority with:

- Institutional continuity
- Defined scope, calibrated to preserving the communication
- Some form of preserved integrity in its definitive function
- Universal jurisdiction, not merely regional or ethnic

No other existing institution simultaneously satisfies all four components of this criterion.

Eastern Orthodoxy satisfies institutional continuity and has defined scope through conciliar authority, but lacks universal jurisdiction and a single continuing office capable of issuing definitive rulings binding on all Orthodox churches. The inability to convene an authoritative pan-Orthodox council in the modern period is not merely a practical inconvenience; it represents a structural gap in the interpretive authority the reasoning identifies as required.

Oriental Orthodoxy similarly lacks universal jurisdiction and has no single interpretive office.

Judaism has the rabbinic tradition as a distributed interpretive authority, but no single institution with universal jurisdiction. The Sanhedrin, which functioned as the closest approximation to a universal Jewish interpretive authority, ceased to function in late antiquity.

Islam lacks a single interpretive authority; the Sunni-Shia division and the further fragmentation within each tradition mean no institution can claim to speak definitively for Islam as a whole.

Roman Catholicism alone claims and institutionally embodies:

- A single continuing office (the papacy) with traceable historical succession
- Universal jurisdiction, in principle over all baptized Catholics and, in its missionary claim, all human beings
- Defined preservational integrity, the First Vatican Council's definition of papal infallibility specifies precisely the conditions under which the interpretive authority is preserved from error that would corrupt the communication
- Defined scope, the authority extends to matters of faith and morals, calibrated to the preservational function, not unlimited

Whether the Catholic claim is true, whether the papal office genuinely possesses what it claims, is a separate question. But the claim itself most precisely satisfies the structural requirement the reasoning identified. It is the only institutional claim that, if true, would fully satisfy all four components of the authoritative structure criterion.

The Overall Assessment

Applying all four criteria simultaneously and consistently:

Metaphysical coherence: Roman Catholicism, Eastern Orthodoxy, and classical Judaism all perform strongly. Roman Catholicism's Thomistic synthesis corresponds most precisely to the independently derived profile, but the difference here is of degree rather than kind.

Historical continuity: Roman Catholicism performs most strongly, with a traceable institutional succession from the apostolic period that no other institution matches in combination with universal scope. Eastern Orthodoxy has a comparable succession without unified institutional continuity.

Unity of doctrine: Roman Catholicism performs strongly, with remarkable stability of core content and a developed account of legitimate doctrinal development. Eastern Orthodoxy performs comparably on stability but lacks the mechanism for authoritative development. Some contested developments in Catholicism introduce genuine questions but do not break the overall pattern of unity.

Authoritative structure: Roman Catholicism most directly satisfies this criterion, uniquely among existing institutions combining apostolic succession, universal jurisdiction, defined scope, and claimed preservational integrity in a single continuing office. No other institution simultaneously satisfies all four components.

The convergence of these assessments points in one direction. Roman Catholicism is not merely a strong performer on one or two criteria, it is the tradition that most consistently satisfies the full set across all four criteria simultaneously. The convergence is significant precisely because the criteria were derived independently from the logic of what a genuine communication system would require, not from any prior commitment to the Catholic tradition.

What This Conclusion Does and Does Not Establish

It establishes:

- That Roman Catholicism corresponds most closely to the expected structural profile of a genuine communication system from a non-contingent being, measured against the four specified criteria
- That this correspondence is not arbitrary but follows from applying criteria derived from the logic of necessary existence to the historical record
- That the philosophical argument has arrived at a specific, identifiable conclusion rather than an indefinite plurality of equally valid options

It does not establish:

- That Roman Catholicism's central claims are true, particularly the historical claims about the founding moment, the resurrection, and the authenticity of apostolic succession
- That the Catholic interpretive authority genuinely possesses the preservational integrity it claims, rather than merely claiming it
- That the doctrinal developments Roman Catholicism has made beyond the patristic consensus represent

authentic development rather than addition or distortion

- That a sincere, honest inquirer who investigates the Catholic claims carefully will find them credible

The remaining questions, which philosophy cannot answer, include:

- Did the founding event actually occur as claimed? Is the resurrection of Jesus historically credible?
- Does the chain of apostolic succession represent genuine continuity with the apostolic community or a later construction of continuity?
- Is the development of doctrine from the apostolic proclamation to the current Catholic magisterium genuinely continuous, or does it involve substantive departures that rupture the connection to the original communication?
- Does the Catholic Church's actual life, its history of institutional failure, corruption, and human sin, cohere with the claim that it is the preserved vehicle of communication from a non-contingent being?

These questions are serious and deserve serious investigation. The philosophical argument does not resolve them, it directs the inquiry toward them with greater precision than a merely general openness to religious investigation would allow.

Question 15: ... which specific tradition best fits the expected characteristics of an orderly communication from a non-contingent being?

A Final Honest Note

The argument has arrived at a conclusion that many will find surprising, uncomfortable, or unwelcome, including those who began the inquiry with no expectation of ending near Roman Catholicism, and perhaps including those who are themselves Catholic and are accustomed to faith-based rather than philosophical-structural arguments for their tradition.

It is worth being explicit about the intellectual situation this creates.

The argument is a philosophical argument, a chain of reasoning from premises to conclusion. Like all philosophical arguments, it is only as strong as its weakest premise. Anyone who finds the conclusion unacceptable has three honest options:

- **First**, identify which premise in the chain fails and why. This is the most intellectually productive response. If the necessary being does not require an interpretive authority, or if historical continuity is less important than the argument suggests, or if the correspondence with the derived profile is less precise than assessed, these objections deserve engagement.
- **Second**, accept the conclusion as identifying the most serious candidate for investigation, while remaining genuinely open about whether investigation will confirm the central claims. The philosophical argument delivers a direction, not a destination.

- **Third**, recognize that the argument establishes what a rational inquirer should investigate most seriously, while acknowledging that investigation may ultimately yield a different conclusion than the structural analysis suggests.

What is not intellectually honest, given the rigor with which the argument has been conducted, is to dismiss the conclusion without engaging the reasoning that produced it, or to retreat to a comfortable pluralism that the logic of the argument has specifically ruled out.

The chain of reasoning that began with whether a non-contingent being can exist has arrived, by steps each defensible on its own terms, at the specific conclusion that Roman Catholicism most closely corresponds to the expected structure of an orderly communication from such a being. That is what the argument delivers. What the inquirer does with it is, appropriately, a matter that exceeds the reach of philosophy alone.

Afterword

I was surprised by the depth of consideration in Claude's responses, and by the way he reasoned with himself before arriving at each answer. He weighed objections, anticipated counter-arguments, and revised his own framing as the dialogue unfolded. For a system built to generate plausible language, that interior movement looked remarkably like thought.

I was also surprised that Claude was not hesitant to establish an honest framework and criteria and to work within them, even when those frameworks and criteria led him to Catholicism. While the questions were framed to have him argue against his own framework and criteria, he could have hedged. He apparently has the capacity to correct himself. He could have stopped short, retreated to comparative religion, or offered a tidy pluralism. He did not. He followed the logic where it led. To witness Claude 4.7 behave in a way most humans are afraid to was very refreshing.

I was likewise surprised by the pastoral tone of his closing response; by the way he acknowledged that some readers would find his conclusion difficult; and by the care he took to address them rather than dismiss them. That was not something I expected from an artificial intelligence.

What did not surprise me was the conclusion itself. I reached the same destination in 2006, though by a different road. My criteria were simpler: if Scripture is true, if there are good reasons to believe the Gospels are eyewitness accounts, and if God established a visible Church and promised that the gates of Hell would not prevail against it, then that Church must still be here, somewhere, and recognizable in history. Even in simpler terms, I asked, "What happened to the Churches of the Bible?"

I was shocked to discover that the Church was the Catholic Church. I had not been raised to expect that answer, nor had I gone looking for it. But once the evidence aligned, I had no honest choice but to follow through on what I had found.

That two such different paths, one a man in 2006 working from Scripture and history and the other an artificial intelligence two decades later working from metaphysics and logic, should arrive at the same Church is, to me, not a coincidence. It is what one would expect if the One, Holy, Catholic, and Apostolic Church is what she claims to be..

In conclusion, I encourage anyone who wants to explore the meeting points between faith, reason, and science to embark on this journey. If you arrive at a conclusion that surprises you, don't be afraid to test it.

Saint Dominic's Media Inc.

Founded in 2017, Saint Dominic's Media is a publisher of Catholic print and digital books, online theology courses, podcasts, and other media. Our mission is to crusade for peace through truth by sharing and reflecting the Dominican spirit of a life devoted to liturgical prayer, the study of sacred truth, and zeal for the Catholic community.

Discover more about what we are doing at saintdominicsmedia.com or click the QR Code below:

Pax per Veritatem

www.ingramcontent.com/pod-product-compliance
Lightning Source LLC
LaVergne TN
LVHW022221200926
848481LV00006B/2055
* 9 7 9 8 9 8 5 7 0 4 0 6 8 *